# SOCIOPATH

The Worst of Both Worlds - How to Detect and
Avoid Psychopaths

(A Crisis of Conscience and Empathy)

**Peter Briley**

Published by Oliver Leish

**Peter Briley**

All Rights Reserved

*Sociopath: The Worst of Both Worlds - How to Detect and Avoid Psychopaths (A Crisis of Conscience and Empathy)*

ISBN 978-1-77485-113-5

Legal & Disclaimer

The information contained in this book is not designed to replace or take the place of any form of medicine or professional medical advice. The information in this book has been provided for educational and entertainment purposes only.

The information contained in this book has been compiled from sources deemed reliable, and it is accurate to the best of the Author's knowledge; however, the Author cannot guarantee its accuracy and validity and cannot be held liable for any errors or omissions. Changes are periodically made to this book. You must consult your doctor or get professional medical advice before using any of the suggested remedies, techniques, or information in this book.

Upon using the information contained in this book, you agree to hold harmless the Author from and against any damages, costs, and expenses, including any legal fees potentially resulting from the application of any of the information provided by this guide. This disclaimer applies to any damages or injury caused by the use and application, whether directly or indirectly, of any advice or information presented, whether for breach of contract, tort, negligence, personal injury, criminal intent, or under any other cause of action.

You agree to accept all risks of using the information presented inside this book. You need to consult a professional medical practitioner in order to ensure you are both able and healthy enough to participate in this program.

# Table of Contents

# Introduction

Psychopathy is defined as a personality disorder that is often characterized with antisocial behavior, lack of remorse or empathy and the lack of inhibition. Out of the many types of personality disorders, psychopathy is perhaps the most difficult to distinguish. People who are psychopathic in nature may appear to be charming and outgoing but they are downright terrifying once they decide to show their true nature.

Psychopathy is a complex personality disorder. In clinical psychology, psychopathy has at least two types of concepts which include the Cleckleyan psychopathy and the criminal psychopathy. The former is defined as someone who is characterized of having bold, uninhibited behavior and low anxiety while the latter is characterized of having a more aggressively persistent behavior often associated with serious criminal behavior. Many people believe that a person who is It is important to discuss the two concepts because many people believe that once a person is labeled as a psychopath, he or she is immediately linked to criminals and murderers. Apparently, many of the convicted serial killers and crime offenders throughout the history showed signs of psychopathy.

Unfortunately, there are no statistics available that indicate the number of people who are suffering from psychopathy in the United States. The reason for this is that the number is underestimated because society has little knowledge about psychopathy and that most people who are categorized as psychopaths are those who were apprehended by the law. Little you may know you might be dealing with a psychopath already. Thus, this book provides a comprehensive guide on how to spot a psychopath as well as learn how to deal with them.

# Chapter 1: Sociopath Defined

Sociopaths are often viewed with extreme prejudice and are often treated as a threat. That is because most people are stuck with the thinking that sociopaths are criminals, serial killers, and generally dangerous people. But, the truth is that most sociopaths live among us and they seem to live normal lives.

The Common Characteristics of Sociopaths One of the first things you should know about sociopaths is that they can be very charming. These are people who are equipped with charisma. This is one of the main characteristics of a sociopath that allows them to draw people in. The glow in their personality gives other people the impression that they can be trusted. Other people tend to go to them for guidance and direction.

Sociopaths have an innocent charisma. But, they are also gifted with sexual appeal, although this does not mean that all sexy people are sociopaths. The sexual appetite of the typical sociopath is rather over the top. They are also likely to have weird fetishes.

As compared to other people, sociopaths are rather spontaneous. They can be very intense, which at times can be mistaken for passion. They are bizarre and are more likely to be erratic. While most people act within the normal social norms and respect social contracts, sociopaths are wary about such things. They are likely to behave in an irrational manner. They often engage in risky behavior.

The feelings of guilt, remorse, and shame are some things that normal people are quite familiar with. A sociopath, on the other hand, lacks these feelings. Their brains that lack the proper circuitry that is capable of processing these emotions.

For this reason, sociopaths find it easy to betray other people. They also find it "normal" to resort to threats. They can even harm others. When they have their mind set on something, they are unlikely to be swayed.

Sociopaths are self serving. Their main concern is their own interests. It does not matter whether they harm people along the way, as long as they get what they want, when they want it. Some people who serve in government positions have this kind of tendency. To them, the end justifies the means.

Sociopaths are likely to be liars. They are in fact, pathological liars. They have no problem inventing truth. They lie about everything, including their experiences. They also exaggerate. They do so to the point of absurdity. But, because they have a gift for storytelling, they are rather believable.

Sociopaths can win people over. They are fixated on the idea of winning. They will not back down in an argument or a fight. Sociopaths will defend their stories and lies viciously. They will do whatever it takes to avoid getting caught in their own web of lies.

These are considered to be highly intelligent people. The problem is, they often use their intelligence for deception. For a sociopath, being able to deceive others gives them some kind of power.

Sociopaths are likely to have high IQs. While this may be a positive thing, the way they decide to use their intelligence is what makes them dangerous. This is proven by those sociopathic serial killers who can evade law enforcement.

Sociopaths are self centered. They do not feel love the way other people do. They lack love and compassion. However, they can fake these emotions in an effort to get what they want and what they think they deserve.

These people also have a gift for words. They speak poetically. Sociopaths are master wordsmiths. Their monologues and speeches can be very hypnotic, and the same time, very intriguing. They are excellent storytellers.

Sociopaths will never apologize for the things they do wrong. They will never admit to any faults. That is because in their minds, they lack such awareness. They feel no guilt and they have no conscience to bother them.

Even if they are confronted with strong evidence, a sociopath will find a way to escape being confronted. Instead of apologizing, a sociopath will resort to an attack that makes the other person feel guilty. They can turn the tables, just like that.

What makes the lies of a sociopath believable is the fact that they believe their own lies. A sociopath can twist the truth with his or her words. They are outstanding at creating illusions.

How to get to the truth?

Sociopaths can create their own truth. They are experts in creating elaborate stories and fictional explanations in an effort to justify their actions. They create illusions.

When a sociopath is caught red-handed, he will deny his guilt and never apologize. Rather, a sociopath will respond with threats and anger. He will then create new lies and invent a more elaborate explanation to get away from being held responsible for what he was caught doing.

For instance, a sociopath who has just been caught with stolen bag full of cash will never admit that he actually stole the money. Instead, he is likely to deny the truth. He would invent a story, for instance, that he is actually saving the money to prevent other people from stealing it. He might say he is trying to give the money back to the rightful owner.

If you did not know any better, you would believe the story and actually declare the thief a hero. Someone who questions the sociopath will be met with an attack. The sociopath is more likely to defend his "honor" and shame you for even questioning his so called honesty.

The lack of conscience, shame, remorse, and guilt makes the sociopath's mind a truly criminal one. The way a sociopath's mind works is perfect for committing and getting away with crimes. They can deceive people, creating arguments and strife. They can make people turn against each other. Sociopaths are extremely delusional. While they may be intelligent, they can defy logical reasoning.

It can be very difficult and even impossible to reason with a sociopath. If you want to find out the truth, you have to ask questions, but you must proceed with caution. Otherwise, you will only drown further in the sociopath's ocean of lies. You should never attempt to reason with this kind of person, unless you want to waste your time. Reasoning with a sociopath will only cause you to annoy him. Trying to reason with this kind of individual is essentially a futile cause.

# Chapter 2: Characteristics Of A Sociopath

Your best friend or your neighbour could be a sociopath; this does not mean they are about to commit a crime, or that there is anything wrong with you. As already mentioned, a sociopath is able to connect with an individual or a small group. They will always be seen as the slightly eccentric member of the group, but, can have long term relations if there is no reason for conflict to occur. Thus is an incredibly brad brush and may mean that one person in the group is regularly patching things up with the sociopath.

In order to recognise a sociopath it is essential to know and understand their main character traits:

- Behaviour

A sociopath will behave according to what they feel is right and best suits their needs and desires. They will usually seek instant gratification and this will often lead to promiscuous behaviour. As they have no interest in the effects of their actions they are happy to have sexual relations at any moment and anywhere. This is not an attempt to grab attention; it is simply the need to satisfy a carnal urge; regardless of where they are or who they are with. Whilst their behaviour can be used to manipulate others; they are usually more subtle than this.

• Feelings

Sociopaths have very few if any feelings on display. This is a direct result of the situations they have been exposed to in life. Despite the building of relations with others you will notice that they never truly feel happy or sad. Where you may celebrate a great victory or even shed a tear at a particularly moving event, they will not. It is possible that they will attempt to emulate your emotion in order to appear part of the group but this will simply be to help them 'fit in'.

It is also possible they will develop feelings of attachment but these feelings and emotions will be shallow, superficial and help them to gain what they need. Unfortunately, a sociopath has no regard for the people and things which surround it and this makes it extremely difficult for them to develop any real feelings. They can become experts at mimicking feelings and this can result in you believing you are helping them and continuing to do so. This is in fact, a clever way of manipulation you to ensure you assist them with whatever they wish to achieve.

- Abide by the Law

As the average sociopath is not interested or even aware of normal social conventions and boundaries they are often found to be on the wrong side of the law. It is highly likely that a sociopath will indulge in law breaking behaviour as they have no regard for the effect of their actions and simply indulge in any kind of behaviour which suits their needs. Often the activities which appear to be the most fun are the ones which are against the law and they will do these activities again and again without fear of the consequences.

- Safety

Unfortunately a sociopath has no real concept of safety. In fact, to most sociopath's safety is not something that even registers as a concern. This does not just apply to their own safety; if their actions are likely to put others at risk, they are highly unlikely to register the danger and take any appropriate action. This is not usually a malicious action but simply a lack of awareness of the risks involved.

- Aggression

A sociopath lives in the moment; this can mean that they will react badly to a variety of situations. In truth their actions are generally completely spontaneous and they can react extremely badly if things do not go as they expect them to. This often translates into aggression. A sociopath is likely to become involved in physical violence and even assault others if they believe that a situation develops does not suit them and their needs. Their aggression will often manifest as threats and verbal abuse before they become violent; in fact, in the majority of cases the threats are enough to make people react how they want them to. This behaviour can be directed at anyone; regardless of whether you consider them a friend or not.

- Spontaneous

This is a key trait of any sociopath. They have an urgent need for instant gratification and this can make them extremely spontaneous. They may wish to try something different through boredom or because they see an opportunity to further their own interests. No matter what the reason they are likely to switch from one activity to another; disregarding any activity and the people that go with it as soon as it loses its appeal. To an onlooker it will appear that the sociopath is capable of starting a wide range of products but is not capable of finishing any project.

This effect is compounded by a sociopath's inability to plan for the future. The need for instant gratification and living in the moment means that they have no time to consider the long term effect and will always fail to plan for the long term.

• Empathy

The lack of emotional response and an inability to appreciate the emotions of others and the effects of their actions is connected with the lack of empathy the typical sociopath displays. A sociopath is unable or unwilling to connect with others and to look at a situation through the eyes of another. This makes it extremely difficult, if not impossible to act in the interest of others. Of course, as a sociopath does not have the ability to connect with others they do not have any issue with acting in any way that suits them. This can be exceptionally convenient and make the decision making process very easy as the only thing which needs to be considered is whether it will make them happy or not.

- Deceitful

When things go wrong a sociopath will happily pass the blame onto someone else; this can result in an issue if the other person does not wish to accept the blame! Creating a lie and building on that lie is something that a sociopath will do without thinking, the lie can be built upon until it is thrown out of all proportion. This will often lead to the exposure of the lie. The true sociopath will probably react with aggression when the lie is uncovered; they will quickly point the blame in a new direction and build a new lie to cover this redirection.

It is important to understand that these lies are a product of a mind which is unable to comprehend the effects of these lies on others. They are not usually deliberately designed to be hurtful; they are simply a means to an end. The usual aim for a sociopath is to establish a comfortable life; their deceit will be motivated by the need for monetary reward. In some cases the deceit will be the result of the need to be accepted, although even this will be part of a larger plan.

Perhaps the most common methods of deceiving people is to object if someone says they do not have good motivation; they will point at the actions they have taken and highlight that these action are helpful to others and illustrate that they are good people. This will probably make you feel guilty for questioning their intent and you will end up doing what they need to remove your own feelings of guilt.

• Sense of Self

Someone who is suffering from an alternative personality disorder, specifically a sociopath, has a heightened sense of their own self worth and that this self-worth is the ultimate motivation for them to pursue any course of action. Their heightened sense of self worth will lead them to seeing others as objects rather than people with needs and desires. This then leads to a lack of understanding of the need for personal space which most people possess.

The sense of self highlights an interesting dilemma that is relevant to sociopaths, even if they are not aware of it themselves. A sociopath will not have a well defined moral identity; their actions are motivated by personal gain and not by the standard moral compass. This means that they will not be able to undertake any lifelong project as their time, patience and motivation will not support such a project. However, it is this type of project which can help anyone to have a more fulfilling, purposeful life. It is these projects which become part of a life and help to define a person and heighten their own self worth. This is something that a sociopath wants to aspire to but they are unable to understand the basic need for personal identity and moral integrity which makes it possible.

- Manipulative

Sociopaths work at a much more simplistic level; they seek to manipulate those around them in order to achieve their own goals. Sociopaths do not have the moral boundaries that the majority of people do have. This means that they are able to use any method available to them to convince you to assist them; even if the method in question is violent.

Although most sociopaths are not good at planning for the future, or even looking past the here and now; they will easily pick up on your fears and desires. Their ability to appear to fit in for short period will enable them to understand your motivation. This can then be used to inspire you and trick you into helping them; either by believing you are making yourself a better person or by believing it will genuinely help the sociopath.

Their manipulation tactics do not need to be malicious although they may be. As they do not understand the effects of their behaviour they are guided by self adulation and not the well being of others.

It is likely that a Sociopath will display all of the above traits and that these traits will have been visible since childhood. Of course, as young people develop many of them will go through 'difficult phases'; this is a normal part of development and can make it hard to spot anyone who has a sociopath personality type as opposed to being a teenager. As someone matures it becomes more obvious, although not easier treat.

Knowing the traits will go a long way towards assisting you spotting one, as already mentioned, it is highly likely that you have already met one and are possibly already being manipulated in ways you did not know were possible!

To assist in avoiding this or in dealing with the situation if it has already arisen then it is essential to read the following guide for additional ways to spot a sociopath;

Charming

The average sociopath is surprisingly charming; they may come across as a valuable member of society who is only interested in helping and supporting others. Unfortunately, there are also plenty of people in life who are genuinely seeking to help others. This makes it exceptionally difficult to know if you are dealing with a genuine person or a sociopath.

One of the best places to start is to examine their 'facts' more closely. A sociopath will be a prevalent liar; if you are prepared to do a little digging you should be able to investigate some of the claims they have made. It will quickly become apparent that they have fabricated the information. Even if a specific outcome has happened it will not have been influenced by the sociopath, unless it suited their needs at the time.

Their ability to charm will probably also extend to an ability to make you feel at ease; they will be excellent at flattering you and you are probably likely to seek out their advice as they will imply they have a huge amount of worldly knowledge to impart.

Attraction

Many sociopaths will appear sexually attractive; this will be a result of their own feelings of self worth which provides them with the appearance of self confidence. It is also the product of a strong sexual appetite. This does not mean that all attractive people are sociopaths; but any with an excessive self-interest and an inability to consider other people's feelings could be!

Competitive

A sociopath will want to win, no matter what the activity. This is because they believe themselves to be better than others; making winning a foregone conclusion. In reality this means that they will do anything to ensure they win, including, but not limited to, things which would be beyond the scope of most people's comprehension.

This is also apparent when someone attempts to destroy the web of lies they have surrounded themselves with. The first reaction will be to build more lies and defend their position; even if they start to contradict themselves. If this approach does not work they are likely to become aggressive and potentially violent. They will never admit to being wrong and a sociopath will never apologise unless they feel it is beneficial to them to do so. Even if this is the case it is likely to be a confusing, story like apology which will make you feel like you have been apologised to when you have, in fact, not actually received an apology!

Wordsmiths

Sociopaths are generally very good with words; this enables them to talk about complex theories and to become excellent storytellers and, often, poets. This ability allows them to transfix the majority of people and dazzle them with their knowledge and command of language. This is usually enough to convince the listener that they know what they are talking about.

In fact, they can often come across as hypnotic; their stories will seem real and will become so intriguing that you will be unable to resist listening to them and becoming absorbed by them.

Heroic

One of the most obvious traits of a sociopath is the ability to be the hero. You probably believe and hope you would do the right thing in a given situation and put other people first, becoming a hero in the process. However, in reality there are very few opportunities where you are faced with these challenges and choices.

A sociopath will have appeared to have been in this situation many times and will have made the right decision to protect others, every time. This is a direct result of the ability to lie at any moment. If they are caught out looking after their own interests they will quickly spin the story to ensure it reflects them as a hero. In fact, many situations which require a hero have actually been created by the sociopath and their inability to see their part in the process compounds this process.

The first rule and the easiest approach when dealing with a suspected sociopath is to check the facts. However, do not ask those who are following the person to verify any information; they will be too under the sociopath's influence. Verify any claim independently, however, you should be cautious when approaching a sociopath with this truth; they will use their mastery of words to turn your own words against you. Sometimes it is better to establish the truth in your own mind and simply walk away.

# Chapter 3: How To Recognize A Sociopath

Sociopathic or psychotic individuals generally have a long standing behavioral pattern which involves the difficulty or even the inability to empathize with other people. They also typically do not have any remorse or any consideration of the rights or feelings of others. These traits allow them to easily deceive, manipulate, and even violate the rights of other people.

Armed with these traits and behaviors, interacting with sociopaths may indeed be dangerous for you or at the very least, make your daily life much more difficult. So how exactly do you recognize or spot a sociopath before you fall prey to one?

To do so, it would be valuable to examine the following red flags of sociopathy as described in Hervey Cleckley's book entitled 'The Mask of Sanity':

High degree of superficial charm and extraordinary intelligence

Most sociopaths are known to be very charming individuals, especially when you first meet them. They are great at charming other people because they know that this is an effective means of getting what they want. Without feeling genuine emotions, they find a way to advance their hidden agenda by effectively learning how to mingle well with others.

With their typically unusual intellect, sociopaths know how to make people feel extremely good about themselves and they can easily fool other people into believing that they are truly interesting and likeable individuals, thus, making it easier for these people to fall into their skillfully devised traps and consequently, to their control and manipulation.

Lack of shame or remorse

Another common trait of a sociopath is the lack of feelings of shame or remorse. They may deliberately hurt others physically or emotionally and not feel the least bit shameful or remorseful of their actions.

However, the sociopath typically will also take none of the blame for any of his life's problems or for the troubles he inflicts on others. Instead, the sociopath will blame everybody else and will even consider his own self to be the victim in the situation.

This lack of shame or remorse is particularly what allows sociopathic individuals to create crimes or unethical behaviors without even having troubled thoughts after the done actions and without even having any difficulties getting a good night's sleep afterwards.

Ability to remain unusually calm in spite of terrible circumstances

Unlike how most people would normally feel, sociopaths typically do not feel nervous or anxious even in the face of terrible circumstances and disturbing situations. Sociopathic individuals do not register events or situations the same way as normal individuals would.

As such, sociopaths hardly generate the same appropriate reactions even in dangerous, scary or highly emotional situations and they are able to maintain extraordinary poise and an eerie sense of calmness even under circumstances which may typically cause agitation, fear, unease, embarrassment, or worry for ordinary individuals.

It has also been found that sociopaths do not get anxious or perturbed when shown extremely disturbing scenes or images even when such things would automatically make other individuals look away under normal circumstances.

Unreliability or Irresponsibility

While they may try to give the impression of being reliable or responsible individuals, it eventually becomes apparent that sociopaths are in fact, unreliable and do not possess a good sense of responsibility in both insignificant and serious matters of their life.

They repeatedly fail to fulfill obligations, promises, and commitments made to other individuals. However, sociopaths may actually mask their irresponsible behaviors by doing various conforming behaviors which may significantly allow them to make a good impression and appear reliable to others.

Even while it can be expected that their failure to realize promises and obligations will continue, it is just plain impossible to exactly foresee when they will happen. Thus, it is extremely difficult to take the suitable precautions against the consequences of the sociopaths' irresponsibility.

No evidence of delusions, irrational thinking, and other signs of a mental illness

Sociopaths do not display any evidence of having a mental illness. They seem to be able to perfectly think and reason logically. They outwardly show nothing odd or strange about them and almost everything they exhibit only suggests something which may in fact be desirable to others. This is considered to be one of the primary reasons why it is particularly hard to recognize if a person is indeed a sociopath.

Sociopathic individuals may also appear to have the ability to respond with normal feelings or emotions and they may even seem to be pretty convincing about their beliefs. But then again, these do not exactly mean that what they are expressing are genuine feelings.

Egocentricity and incapacity for love

Being egocentric or self-centered is one of the key aspects of being a sociopath. At times, sociopaths may effectively hide their egocentricity. However, upon thorough observation of their behaviors, such trait is considered to be fixed and absolute. The degree of this particular trait can indeed be beyond belief and it may even be best expressed as incapacity or the failure to love.

Despite this incapacity however, sociopaths are well known for their ability to mimic behavior. This allows them to skillfully pretend to love others, especially those who may prove to be beneficial for their own goals and purposes, once again pointing to their egocentricity.

Insufficiently motivated antisocial behaviors

Sociopaths may swindle, forge documents, do fraudulent acts, get into brawls, and other do other acts generally unacceptable by society even when there is a great risk of being discovered and even when there is no sufficient motivation for such acts.

These behaviors are not limited as well. Sociopaths may engage in a wide range of activities which tend to hurt and violate the rights of others around them.

Untruthfulness and insincerity

Sociopaths are excellent liars. They exhibit such an extraordinary disregard for truth and they have the ability to easily weave lies very convincingly even when looking somebody straight into the eye.

They are very much capable of showing no physical signs of discomfort and can seem pretty straightforward even while telling lies and this usually results to the other person completely believing and being convinced by the sociopaths' web of deceit.

And whether or not there is a high risk of getting caught, sociopaths will display the same remarkable abilities of lying. They will lie about anything, anytime, and usually even for no good reason at all.

Poor judgment and failure to learn from previous experiences

Despite their typically high levels of intellect, sociopathic individuals are often known for having poor judgment and failing to learn from previous experiences. They often dispose of wonderful opportunities, such as building and improving personal relationships.

Despite punishments for previously enacted wrong behaviors, they will also typically continue displaying the same behavior even if they know that doing such will again lead to receiving punishment.

In certain theoretical circumstances, they may be able offer sensible pieces of advice to others. But then again, when it comes to taking action, evidences of poor decision making may then become more apparent.

Lack of major affective reactions or emotions

Generally, sociopaths are incapable of feeling genuine emotions. They may learn verbal descriptions of certain feelings and may even mimic other people as to how such emotions are displayed.

However, sociopathic individuals are in reality not able to feel deep joy, real despair, genuine empathy, and many other emotions typically felt by ordinary people. They may act as if they have these feelings but only to such extent. Nothing is ever truly genuine.

Lack of response in general interpersonal relations

Sociopathic individuals do not typically respond to acts of kindness or to trust given to them. Even when they are treated very well, they will never feel any obligation over giving back the same positive treatment as appreciation to the other person.

But sociopaths may carry out acts of small favors to others. This is, however, not out of appreciation or any feelings of longing to help. Usually, such acts are carried out in order to elicit a sense of obligation in the individual who is receiving the favor or they do it simply to create a good impression.

Sociopaths may see such behaviors as something which may significantly make it easier to control or manipulate the individual who is on the receiving end of the favor.

Shocking, fantastic and uninviting behaviors that come with drinking and sometimes without

Some sociopaths are known not to drink. However, some others are also known to frequently indulge in drinking and when they do, it elicits shocking, fantastic and uninviting behaviors.

Highly offensive behaviors may rise, as well as, ill-treatments to others, especially their wife or children. Sudden and immediate shifts between being over-sentimental and being conceited may also be exhibited by the sociopath. There is rarely any genuine cheerfulness, real warmth and friendliness, or any proof of pleasurable reactions.

However, the alcohol may numb the sociopaths' inhibitions and then give rise to strange and outlandish behaviors. This may lead to them doing acts which ordinary people typically would not even think of doing. Even a little amount of alcohol may already trigger these behaviors.

Before indulging in drinking, they may completely be aware of what they have done in the past associated to it but proceed to drinking anyway.

Specific loss of insight

Despite their typically high intellect, sociopaths do not have the ability to see themselves in the exact way others see them. They also do not have the ability to know exactly how other people feel upon seeing them or upon being exposed to their presence.

They are known to have a specific loss of insight especially when it comes to matters about emotions. But despite this inability, they can still pretend, mainly because they have read about it. They can use the words and define the feelings. But in reality, they remain blind to what they truly mean.

Suicide threats which are seldom carried out

Suicide threats are typically used by sociopaths in order to manipulate and control others. They may make occasional fake attempts of ending their lives but then again, these are just done for the aim of controlling others. And more often than not, such attempts are found to be premeditated.

Impersonal, insignificant, and poorly integrated sex life

There are consistent peculiarities in the sex life of sociopaths. Like in other areas of their life, it only needs a little amount of impulse for them to already engage in unusual sexual acts and behaviors.

Again, it is very important to take note of the fact that sociopaths are incapable of loving. Thus, any sexual activities they get into do not seem to include anything emotionally meaningful to them. These activities are considered to be plainly limited to the temporary sensations that come with physical contact and nothing of the intimate and emotional facets that typically come with the act.

However, it is very likely that sociopaths realize that intimate sexual contact can be a great way to easily manipulate and control others. And indeed, such acts are often effectively used as a perfect tool which can be used against others.

Failure to follow any life plan

Despite the impression of having high intellectual skills and remarkably desirable characteristics, sociopaths have the inability to consistently follow any of their life plans. They may have a wide range of great ideas. However, they may also have an extreme difficulty in carrying out or performing any of them.

# Chapter 4: Is Your Significant Other

# A Sociopath?

Are you in a relationship with someone who seems too good to be true? Are they so energetic and perfect every second of the day? Maybe everything they say couldn't be more perfect. If you find yourself questioning whether or not this person is the real thing and if they're real well you may be asking yourself these questions for a reason. There are individuals who are sweet and charming and honest while others may be faking their personality in order to fool others. While there are genuine individuals out there, many people who seem to be too perfect usually are. There are qualities in individuals that may make them seem perfect to you, but the reality is that no one is perfect, we all have our flaws.

However, do not confuse a nice and sweet person with a sociopath. It's important to remember that there's a huge difference between someone who lives an honest life and shows an immense amount of others and someone who is faking all of these things in order to fool someone. It's when someone says and does all the right things consistently for a long period of time when red flags start to become present. If you're fairly good at reading people, you may start to suspect after some time that someone seems off. You may start to question whether or not you're being lied to.

Are you concerned that your significant other may be a sociopath? Well, he or she very well might be. In order to clearly identify whether or not this is the case, you must be able to understand what it means to be a sociopath. After going through the signs and characteristics of a sociopath, you probably have a good idea of what it means to be a sociopath. While this may be the case, you may still be unsure if the person you are dating actually falls under this category. It's important to understand specific signs that may be noticeable in a relationship. If the relationship starts off with stories that you feel are fabricated, such as stories that you feel are being told to be more than what they are, they take note of this. Maybe your significant other has expressed to you what a great childhood they had and they go into detail about what they experienced, well if the stories seem to not match up and they change from one thing to the next, then this is a huge red flag. Now keep in mind that some individuals are embarrassed of their upbringing and childhood and may tell lies in order to prevent embarrassment. Make sure that you are aware of all the signs of a sociopath before you start to diagnose your partner who may be telling lies in order to protect themselves from the pain of severe embarrassment.

Along with telling a great deal of lies, sociopaths also tend to try and pull you away from others whom you are close with. Your partner may try and pull you away from your friends and family for no apparent reason, simply because they want you all to themselves. If you find yourself becoming more and more distant from your family after being in a relationship with this person, take a step back and identify why this may be the case. If you start to realize that your significant other may be what's holding you back from your previous relationships, try and understand why this is happening. Now, this may be happening because you're choosing to spend the majority of your time with your new found love, but it may also be happening because your partner is purposely trying to sabotage your close relationships not only to cause you pain but to keep you all to themselves. Sociopaths often manipulate situations so much so that they are able to pull their victims away from those who are close to them. They may make up lies, fabricate stories and tell you things about your friends and family that haven't happened in order to make you believe them and only want to be with them.

For example, maybe your significant other told you that she had a conversation with your mother and your mother expressed nothing but disappointment with the person that you've become. She may run home to you and tell you this story and make sure you know how proud she is of you and that she thinks you're great. This story will be fabricated in order to make you lose trust and respect for your mom. You will then become closer to your girlfriend because she loves you and respects you for who you are even when your family doesn't. When something like this is done, it's done to pull you away from those who truly love you and care about you. Unfortunately, when this happens, it often takes a great deal of time to uncover the lies that you've been told. If you find your significant other consistently telling you negative stories about those around you, keep an eye on this. While it's healthy to share stories of actual events, it is incredibly dysfunctional to fabricate stories in order to make things go your way.

While they may continue to lie in order to make you believe them, even when they know you're feeling hurt and you're upset because of the lies they've told, they will not feel any remorse. Part of this personality disorder is the complete lack of empathy. Sociopaths are able to conduct thee behaviors, lie, cheat, steal and even manipulate entire families without ever feeling any kind of remorse. If for example, a lie such as the one mentioned above is told, no matter what kind of outcome or pain is caused based on this lie, the sociopath will not feel any bit of remorse. An entire relationship between a son and his mother may be ruined forever because of the lie she told but she will never feel bad about this and she will never regret it. When you see this lack of empathy from others, you automatically know that there is a larger problem with this person. The lack of empathy in a relationship is incredibly disturbing. Keep in mind that someone can lack empathy but still be able to cry on cue when needed. Crying, tears and other faked emotions may be very misleading. You may want to assume that if someone is crying that they're feeling real feelings, they may actually feel sorry about what they've done. Do not be fooled! They don't! Sociopaths want you to believe every single lie they tell, even if that lie only involves fake tears and a few sobbing noises every now and then. These individuals are good fakers and good actors. They can make you believe that they are feeling things that they really aren't. The unfortunate thing about this is that when someone cries, it often makes others believe that they really are sad or upset, especially if this is someone that you're dating and that you feel close with.

# Chapter 5: Histrionic Personality Disorder – The Symptoms, Treatment Options And Future Prospects

This personality disorder fits into the B category; it is symptomatic of those who are extremely dramatic and highly emotional. People suffering with this disorder are likely to be very attention seeking and will happily indulge in more and more outlandish and ridiculous behaviour to ensure they remain the focus of the group.

Behaviour

Their outlandish behaviour will keep them centre focus of any group. But if they are not the main focus, for any reason, they will be extremely uncomfortable; this is the time when they are most likely to do something particularly mad.

One tool which is often used to ensure the focus remains on them is sexually seductive behaviour. They will deliberately flirt outrageously and lead people on to attract attention and controversy; this will ensure they are the centre of attention.

Their behaviour will always be a source of conversation and they will always have lively and interesting stories to tell and ideas to follow through on.

Intimacy

People with this disorder usually have intimacy issues. They will also struggle to build friendships with others, particularly those of the same sex. Much of this is connected with their outlandish behaviour as they will be seen as a threat to their friend's relationships. Their desire to be the centre of attention is often conveyed through their sexual provocative behaviour and this is usually seen as a threat. It is also highly likely that their behaviour and need for constant attention will cause a rift with any friends as they will not respect the fact that a couple need time to themselves.

People with this disorder can also struggle to achieve any kind of emotional intimacy with someone they care for. This is because they will often act out a role rather than allowing someone to become close to the real them. This role can be anything from a princess to a victim and may well be part of a plan to manipulate and control their partner through sexual and emotional means. However, they may also display a conflicting need to be looked after by their partner. This can make it extremely difficult for anyone to become close enough to them to understand who they really are.

Stimulation

The need to be the centre of attention extends into every aspect of their life and this can easily translate into a constant need for new experiences; they are likely to crave stimulation and the adrenaline rush of doing something new. Novelty holds a great deal of appeal and sufferers of this disorder are liable to become bored easily. This issue can become a serious problem if they have managed to engage in a relationship as they are generally not interested in waiting for their pleasure. If something does not provide instant gratification they will become frustrated and probably indulge in some, over the top, activity which will give them the instant gratification they desire.

Sadly, their active minds are able to conceive of many brilliant ideas but they will often start a project with great enthusiasm and then quickly get bored and move onto something else.

The need for something exciting and instant is of particularly concern as any relationship will suffer if a new prospect arises. They will switch allegiances at the drop of a hat.

Relationships are often damaged in their early stages as someone with this condition will read much more into the relationship at an early stage than there actually is. Despite their behaviour they will believe they are in an intimate relationship from day one. This behaviour alone can be enough to drive a partner away.

Shallow

The general perception of someone who has a histrionic personality is of someone who is shallow and self-centred. Their emotions are expressed easily but not truthfully, this is usually done to manipulate those around them and achieve the instant gratification they desire.

This conception is usually backed up by the use of their physical appearance to gather attention at every opportunity they can. Their behaviour is generally theatrical and many gestures are exaggerated or overly dramatic.

Even their speech is often dramatic and impressionist without actually providing any real information.

Lead

Despite the fact that people with this disorder love to be the centre of attention and behave madly, they are actually very easily led. This is connected with their desire to be liked and appreciated. They are open to suggestions from others and will often do something just to prove it is possible.

This disorder is more likely to affect a female than a male and the majority of the symptoms will naturally decrease as they age.

Recognising that someone has this issue is the first step to a proper diagnosis and treatment. As already mentioned in this book, a proper diagnosis should be obtained from a professional, although you may have a clear idea of which personality disorder is likely to be the culprit. The only way to be diagnosed with this condition is or a health professional to match your symptoms with the ones described and view these in conjunction with your life history.

Treatment Options

Most people with a personality disorder do not seek treatment unless their symptoms start to affect their ability to live a normal life. Those with Histrionic personality disorder are likely to be one of the first to consult a specialist as they will have pleasure in exaggerating their symptoms and the complications it is causing them. Unfortunately their need for attention will also make it very difficult for them to end their treatment; this is also a reflection of their emotional needs, something that many people do not appreciate that they have.

The standard course of treatment will involve psychotherapy; however, it is not advisable to undertake group session as this will play to their desire to be the centre of attention. One to one treatment is the best option although this may increase the emotional neediness of the sufferer and reluctance to finish therapy.

As most people with this disorder are sexually promiscuous it is essential for a psychotherapist to provide clear boundaries at the start of the treatment and to reinforce these regularly. It is likely that the sufferer will find any medical professional desirable at some point and they will need to be gently reminded of the boundaries. A psychotherapist is also likely to become the daily rescuer for the sufferer. This means they will hear every issue they have, usually in an overly dramatic way and the medical professional will become a supportive figure; this will alleviate some of the pressure and stress on the sufferer's loved ones.

As with any personality disorder there is not a magic pill which will make someone better. Treating someone with Histrionic disorder is a long, slow process. The best approach has been to keep treatment focused on short term goals which are obtainable. These goals should be based on things which will give an immediate benefit to a sufferer's life and a relatively quick solution will appeal to their desire for instant gratification.

The desire to be centre of attention can often manifest itself by stating an intention to attempt suicide. In the majority of cases this, or even an attempt, is designed to obtain attention and not an actual desire to commit suicide. However, sometimes a sufferer can commit suicide when they were only intending to make a statement. This is why it is essential for the therapist to establish a suicide risk analysis and agree with the sufferer when they should contact the therapist. An alternative to this is self-mutilation.

A therapist needs to sift through the exaggerations and build a picture of the sufferer and, ultimately, identify the expectations and fears which drive the sufferer to behave and think in such a way. These expectations and fears are usually impossible to achieve and are the result of years of misconceptions. A therapist will need to underline the fact that this type of behaviour leads to a belief that style is more important than substance. This should be backed up by illustrating which behavioural patterns of the sufferer is a result of these beliefs, and suggesting some alternatives to try. Sufferers who attempt behavioural modification following these sessions are well on the road to recovery. A good therapist will also illustrate the times when a sufferer uses shallow criteria to judge others and adjust their attitude accordingly. Eventually, if a person with this disorder practices assessing when they are being shallow, they will be able to stop themselves from judging others harshly.

Research has shown that cognitive orientated approaches do not have much effect on patients with this disorder; this is mainly due to the inability of sufferers to examine their own feelings and thoughts or even their unconscious motivations. Whilst adding this approach to any treatment plan will not harm the treatment it is unlikely to help in any way.

Of all the personality disorders this is the easiest one to live a relatively normal life with and this can cause some medical professionals to discriminate against sufferers. It is important for any doctor or medical specialist to remain professional at all times, regardless of their own feelings.

The Long term Prospects of Sufferers

With a good supportive network and treatment from a medical professional it is possible to adapt a sufferer's thoughts and feelings to ensure they live a productive, happy life without suicidal thoughts or a dependency on others. People with this disorder should be able to:

Work

Holding down a job can be difficult for many people who suffer with a personality disorder; without a regular income it can be hard to stay on top of all the bills and live an independent life. Many sufferers struggle to maintain their employment due to their anxious and paranoid personalities.

This is not usually an issue for those who are suffering with histrionic disorder. People with this disorder will generally be relatively popular; although they will also be seen as shallow and not worth building a deep friendship with. Their job only comes under threat when their attention seeking behaviour goes a step too far and the management are forced to react.

Regular sessions with the psychotherapist will ensure someone with this disorder learns where the boundaries of normal, socially acceptable behaviour are. It can still take a huge effort to ensure they stay within these boundaries and channel their need to be the centre of attention. A therapist can suggest ways of changing their behaviour and reactions to help them feel like the focus is on them without resorting to extreme stunts.

Friends

Because people with this disorder expend all their energy on being noticed, they have little time for the needs of others. This is the core reason they come across as shallow and are unable to make new friends. Regular therapy sessions will ensure they learn to address these issues by re-focusing their behaviour and attention on those around them and sharing the limelight. This is not an easy process and can be very challenging for someone suffering from this disorder; the desire to be the centre of attention is very strong!

However, by slowly moving the goals; it is possible for any sufferer to learn to let others have their opportunity in the centre. Their desires may always push them to be the centre of attention but they can learn to deal with these and build true friendships with people. Providing they are not too needy or reliant on these new friends they can create and build friendships; this will help them to feel appreciated and lead a more independent life.

New people

Meeting new people appears easy for those with this disorder as they are naturally flamboyant and enjoy the excitement of something or someone new. However, new people are actually a challenge and provide the opportunity for a sufferer to be even more outrageous than normal to ensure they are the centre of attention with these, unknown, quantities.

Therapy can help people with this disorder to understand and manage their expectations in respect of other people and how to interact with them without needing to take centre stage. Much of the focus of the therapy is enabling a sufferer to accept their own self worth without the need for others to confirm this.

This is not an easy thing to teach and the process can take a considerable amount of time. Whilst the fundamental aspects of their personality cannot be changed the approach which a sufferer adopts can be; it is this which can make a huge difference to their quality of life and even allow them to make new friends.

Build Relationships

The majority of people with this disorder will have intimacy issues; these may be deep seated and be a result of actions or experiences when they were young. This is not an easy area to treat in any patient. Behavioural practice can improve the issues listed above and help a sufferer to live a normal life. However, it is likely that they will always struggle with intimacy issues. Their need for reassurance and to be the centre of attention will hinder any relationship; even the most understanding and patient of people will struggle with this aspect of a sufferer's personality.

Therapy should offer some assistance with building relationships but it is unlikely that it will be enough by itself to enable someone with this disorder to build a long term, supportive and two way relationship. Sufferers may need to focus on building friendships and not concern themselves with intimacy until they are better placed to share the limelight.

Adventure seeking

The constant need to be the centre of attention will always be an issue to those with a histrionic personality disorder. The focus of therapy sessions in relation to this should be on how to learn to control their impulses. Poor impulse control is the reason why a sufferer will undertake mad tasks without a thought of the consequences. Learning to control these impulses, without denying them is an essential part to understanding their own personality and cutting down on their shallow, attention seeking behaviour.

The desire to seek new things and want instant gratification may never be removed from their psyche completely; the therapist's role is to ensure they start delaying the gratification, even if they start small by just delaying it for a few seconds. Small, short term goals are the best way to teach these skills and help to improve their overall quality of life.

Risk of depression

Anyone suffering from histrionic disease is at risk of depression; this may seem surprising as they love to be the centre of attention and are generally shallow and excitement seeking. However, it is this constant pressure to be the best and the focus of any room that can lead to depression and anxiety, this is particularly relevant if they are not the centre of attention for an extended period of time.

This part of the personality disorder can be extremely difficult to treat. There is no rule or standard regarding how and when someone will feel depressed and it is not easy for a therapist to install a sense of self-worth in a sufferer which will allow them to feel good about themselves regardless of the attention of others.

The long term goal for this should be to teach the sufferer how to deal with disappointment and why they do not always need to be the centre of attention. This will assist in preventing depression and, potentially, suicidal thoughts.

Treating someone with histrionic disorder will usually take approximately three years; the challenge during this time is keeping it interesting and varied enough to ensure the patient keeps returning. However, although treatment can vastly improve the quality of a sufferer's life, it is essential to educate the family and any close friends to ensure they are able to monitor the sufferer for life; it is that big a commitment.

# Chapter 6: A Psychopath 'In Love'

"Some werewolves are hairy on the inside."

— Stephen King, Danse Macabre

Most psychopaths target either one or multiple partners to satisfy their needs for companionship and connection. While a relationship with a psychopath is an unfortunate one by default, it's essential to know that they act on their own perception of love. As they dread loneliness and isolation, psychopaths resort to manipulation to secure that their partner will stay by their side. The following sections will further explain how psychopaths act in relationships, divorce, and confrontation, and what you can do to protect yourself when you're trying to end a relationship.

## Psychopathic Romance: How They Operate

The misperception of psychopathy in society can easily result in missing the initial signs. You might think of a psychopath as someone who acts like a loner or stands out from the crowd. You'd think your date couldn't possibly be a psychopath because they're smart and confident. However, it is the exact opposite. Psychopaths can be well integrated into society. In addition, there's also a broad spectrum of this condition that makes it hard to pinpoint the exact symptoms. In other mental disorders, the underlying causes lead to symptoms, which then lead to maladjusted behaviors. In psychopathy, the actions are the symptoms of the disorder. Because of this, understanding the psychopath's motives is challenging. The most important thing to note is that in a relationship, a psychopath acts on their own distorted idea of love and companionship.

While their actions cause harm to their partner's health and self-esteem, they're driven by the desire to secure that the partner will never leave. It is a selfish desire, stripped of consideration for the other person. However, understanding the psychopath's motivation will help you understand the profound fear of loneliness that drove them to hurt you. There are a couple of typical behaviors that set psychopaths apart from most people when it comes to relationships. Knowing the psychopath's typical behavioral patterns will help you become resilient to their influence. Here are the most common traits of psychopaths in relationships:

1. They move fast

Psychopaths move fast through relationships, particularly in the early stages. They do this because they fear their partner will slip away. They will move quickly to sex, moving in together, getting married, and having children. Their spouses and partners will be unaware of the personality disorder because they are good at hiding their dark side. In the beginning, they can be fun and attractive.

2. They're deceitful

Psychopaths are prone to not only arrogance and dominance but also deception and gaslighting. Psychopaths reveal their dark side once they are sure that the target has bonded to them. This can happen after a couple of months or even years. Psychopaths are deceitful with the purpose of controlling the image of them you have in your mind. At the same time, they work to lower your self-esteem. They do this because they believe that the only way you'll stay by their side is if you have no one to turn to and nowhere else to go. Within the value system of a psychopath, they can be strong only if you're weak, and you'll stay by their side only when you're broken and hopeless.

3. They're controlling and possessive

Recognizing a psychopath is difficult, but predicting and understanding their actions is next to impossible. It's a lot better for you to focus on the way the person is making you feel instead of their own behavior. Recognizing a psychopath is that much more difficult because they put on a show of someone successful and confident. What's particularly interesting about psychopaths is that their thought process is slightly different than an average person's. It is a lot more hateful, angry, and filled with the desire to control and oppress.

4. They're demanding

It's impossible to make a psychopath happy. In a relationship, they'll be overly critical and demanding to keep you on edge. They want your focus entirely on them, and they'll make sure to occupy your attention with constant remarks. In high-functioning or borderline psychopathic personalities, these dark desires can be unconscious. They might actually think that they are helping you by controlling your life. They may think of you as their project and give up on you once you prove too weak to measure up to their standards. This way of thinking is common in psychopathic parents, and also in high-functioning psychopaths who feel like a partner is their trophy to show off. As such, they might push you beyond your limits, only to abandon you if you can't handle their criticism.

Psychopaths and Divorce

Divorcing a psychopath is not easy, but can that be achieved with only a little damage. The experience itself is most often devastating, heartbreaking and frustrating because their actions are filled with slander, manipulation and low blows. They are also unpredictable. While an average person can understand why someone would not want to be with them, psychopath sees that as a great insult to their ego. To them, a divorce is a game in which they will want to win at all costs. The purpose of the divorce isn't to obtain assets or be correct in the face of justice, but instead to make you suffer and win the game.

How psychopaths act in divorce and in battle for custody

Psychopaths will fiercely battle for custody even though they are not really interested in children. The purpose of a custody battle isn't to get the children, but to hurt you by belittling you as a parent. Their passive-aggressive acts are tools to win the game and make you suffer. They will fight for every penny they can get. Particularly, they will fight for the things they know are meaningful to you. For example, if you want to stay in your home and you are willing to pay them off, they will not accept it. They will not accept any negotiations because their goal is to hurt you.

How to survive a divorce from a psychopath

Psychopaths are unable to understand the reasoning of someone who can make emotional contact for two reasons:

• They agree with anti-social rules because they see the world as an enemy.

• They filter the information in their mind to measure winning versus losing or being powerful versus being weak.

Because of this, reaching an agreement in divorce is going to be extremely difficult. However, there are a number of things you can do to preserve your health throughout the divorce and avoid further abuse from a psychopath:

1.  Cut all ties

The first tip to divorcing the psychopath is to prevent any engagement. Avoid feeding into their drama and instead allow things to unravel on their own. Now, more than ever, you benefit from acting like your abuser tried to train you: being a passive observer. Like a toddler having a tantrum, your future ex will rage and splash money on legal procedures, only to give up when they see they're not affecting you.

Whenever a psychopath notices that something they say or do touches you, they will do it even more. If they are trying to contact you, simply avoid talking to them. Everything you hear from them is going to be lies, manipulation, or threats. If they try to persuade you that they will change, it's a lie. If they threaten, they might only do it to upset you, but make sure to stay safe. If they throw insults and low blows it's only to harm yourself-esteem. For this reason, abandon all contact.

2. Monitor and record

The next piece of advice is to document everything about your life and communication with the psychopath. Although it's less likely that a person without a history of violence will suddenly become violent, it's possible. If you can, record all of your digital activities and install surveillance in your home. Also, record all of your phone conversations, not just with the psychopath. This will serve as proof of your activities in case of slander and false accusations.

For example, if a psychopath accuses you of making threats, the evidence of your own activity can prove your alibi. Recording psychopath's threats, insults, verbal and other attacks is essential, but tracking your own activities ensures that the predator can't touch you without being recorded.

3.  Resist slander and lawyer up

The psychopath will do their best to slander your reputation. You can sue them for that by providing evidence that their allegations are false and that they caused damage to your life and career. You can also use your own evidence to prove that your ex is a pathological liar, which will help in case of a custody battle. If you fear physical violence, or you're afraid that the psychopath might attack you, do everything you can to always have company. Also, make sure to install surveillance into your car, in front of your home, and inside your backyard. GPS devices and cameras are cheap and they can be useful in case the psychopath is following you. You can use this evidence to prove that they are stalking you.

4. Don't give them ammunition

Make sure that the psychopath loses interest in you. The less they know about your life, the less they're able to hurt you. Avoiding contact and not engaging can be successful with some psychopaths, but not all. Some psychopaths my feel irritated by being ignored.

Since you don't benefit from either irritating the psychopath or feeding into their drama, the best thing you can do is to try to make yourself look boring to them. Becoming boring in all aspects of life means to temporarily stop posting content on social media or talking to mutual friends. Instruct your friends and family to avoid talking to your ex. And if they have to, tell them not to share anything about your life that might be interesting to this person.

5.   Avoid judging yourself negatively.

Understand that their behavior is solely their fault. You've been targeted because of your kind and perhaps impressionable nature. However, that doesn't mean that there is anything wrong with you and that your qualities are flaws. Appreciate your own good qualities and don't let yourself see them as a weakness.

Accept that emotional healing is going to take a lot of time. It could take years depending on the severity of the abuse, or whether or not there was physical or sexual abuse involved. You should be patient with your own healing. The emotional damage and the damage to your sense of self-worth is enough, let alone surviving violent abuse. Don't blame yourself for being unable to recover fast and don't push yourself into recovery.

## 6. Stop trying to be right

The next tip is to let go of trying to prove your point. People who are outside your marriage may fall under the influence of your psychopathic ex. They may believe their story. Or they may think that you made a mistake for divorcing them. The same way you shouldn't engage with your ex, you shouldn't engage with others' views on your divorce either. If these people aren't significant to you, let them go from your life. Don't try to explain to people your side of the story if they are unreceptive of it. More importantly, let go of the desire for others to support you in your divorce.

## 7. Look for a supportive environment

Oftentimes, it is the person who decides to divorce that receives the most judgment. You are facing the blame for not putting in enough work into preserving the marriage. Some environments go as far as justifying physical violence in relationships and advising people, women in particular, to endure through this abuse for the sake of marriage. In the eyes of many, nothing that happens in a marriage justifies a divorce. Accept that some people are simply narrow-minded, but they are not the ones who make decisions in your life. You are the only one who does that.

8.   Review and reflect

It's important to reflect on the experience so that you can fully understand what happened. Get clarification whenever you can. The more you learn about psychopaths and about ways to recover from them, the easier it will be for you to accept your reality. Get all the support you can and do the best you can to focus on your own personal recovery and growth instead of the other person. Practice mindfulness and self-healing to enforce your self-esteem and independence. Psychopaths and Confrontation

You've most likely encountered many psychopaths without knowing. The reason that you haven't suffered the same amount of damage from them as you did from your ex is that you didn't engage much. In confrontation, psychopaths are Machiavellian manipulators. Their goal is to win. You can't count on reasoning with a psychopath because they don't care. They care neither about the truth nor the effects of their actions. To a psychopath, your pain and anger are rewarding. Their ultimate goal is to see you suffer. Here's what you can expect in confrontation with a psychopath:

Unpredictable

A psychopath is unpredictable in conflict. Forget about obsessing and trying to predict what they will say or do, and instead focus on yourself and prevent them from causing more damage. If you are worried about their aggressive behavior, instead of accusing them of it, secure your home and yourself. In confrontation, a psychopath's only goal is to get what they want. They do this by using all of your weaknesses against you. They know what you need at the moment and they will use that against you.

Ambiguous

They will use conflicting messages to cloud your judgment. They will do their best to ruin your life by ruining your relationships and your work. If you are trying to get some distance from a psychopath, and they don't want to let you go, they will resort to all sorts of slander as a way of causing harm to your life.

How to Stay Safe

Either working or being in a relationship with a psychopath can be distressing and toxic. Psychopaths create a toxic environment by inducing stress in others and preying upon their character weaknesses. For example, if you have self-esteem issues, they might boost your self-esteem to gain your trust but then do their best to ruin it once you trust them.

While successful psychopaths tend to be callous, dishonest, and arrogant in nature, they can still put on a pleasant face. However, after this, they will be prone to exploiting others, placing the blame on anyone else but themselves, and imposing themselves on others. They will do their best to take credit for others' successes. Depending on the level of psychopathy, psychopaths can also rank higher or lower in level of consciousness. Successful psychopaths tend to act less irresponsible, negligent, and impulsive. However, that doesn't make them less dangerous. That simply means that they will spend more time planning directions and recording your weaknesses. Here are a couple of suggestions for you to stay safe when you can't avoid being around a psychopath:

1. Focus on your emotions

You can't affect a psychopath's thought process or their behavior, but you can focus on the way you feel. You can take away a psychopath's power over you by acknowledging that the way they make you feel is as an exaggerated expression of your insecurities.

2. Be brave

Losing your temper with a psychopath only feeds into their ego. Don't show fear. Psychopaths use fear as a source of control. They will make threats, stalk, slander, and do everything they can to intimidate you. Stay safe, but don't let them see that you are affected. It may not be the safest to say that they make empty threats. Regardless, don't show any fear, and don't let their stories affect you. If you are in the midst of a conflict with a psychopath, don't let anything they say get inside your head before you fact check it.

3. Point out their flaws

When you are forced to talk to a psychopath with whom you're in a conflict, gather factual evidence of their mistakes. If it's a divorce, collect factual proof of abuse, negligence, and responsibility. When confronted with this evidence that psychopaths will lose their power.

4. Build up your mental power

Work on your own mental strength, employing all of your resources and energy into making your headspace solely your own. Moreover, focus all of your efforts into nurturing independence. Codependency made you vulnerable to abuse, to begin with, and only by healing it will you be able to recover truly.

5. Don't provoke them

Aside from avoiding engagement, avoid getting in a verbal argument with a psychopath. Arguments with a psychopath don't have any chance of success and verbal provocation can easily spark a violent outburst. Only communicate with your ex through your lawyer. It is recommended to do that by delivering the information without asking questions.

6. Monitor their actions

Focus on their actions and not their words. If a psychopath is using painful words, threats, and accusations against you, take these seriously and report them, but with the same emotional cool they treated you with. If you're trying to determine whether or not a psychopath will act on their threats, look into their actions.

7. Be diplomatic

If you want to successfully reach an agreement with a psychopath, you will have to make a win-win agreement. You have to use arguments that make them feel like they are winning in the game.

8. Avoid meeting them

Avoid face-to-face communication with an abusive ex. Psychopaths are only successful in getting what they want through direct communication. Keeping your conversations digital ensures that you have the conversations on record, and strips the abuses of their manipulative powers.

## Chapter 7: How To Deal With A Psychopath

By now, with any luck, you have learned to tell the signs and know that you really are dealing with a bona fide psychopath. Diagnosis is very difficult, from your point of view or from that of a doctor or health care provider. It can also be very hard for you to accept that the person you trusted is not the person you thought he or she was. So how do you deal with a psychopath once you have determined that you are involved with one?

First of you must be a strong person. You have to accept wholly that you are dealing with a person who is a psychopath and until you can do that, you cannot deal with them effectively. Please, do not confuse a psychopath with a serial killer – they don't all go on to commit heinous crimes. In fact, only one in every 30,000 psychopaths will go on to become a serial killer. You must be prepared for the journey ahead of you – it is not going to be easy.

Drop all Contact

The very first thing you must do is stop all contact with the psychopath in your life. Yes, this is easier said than done, I know. They have been a big part of your life for some time and just dropping away them from altogether will be tough. How tough will depend entirely on how deep your relationship was. If you only met recently, it will be easier than if you have been together for some time. To cut all contact though, you must take physical action to stop all communications and interactions.

Keep it Quiet

Don't announce your intentions to all and sundry. Be cautious and quiet about stopping interaction with the psychopath. Do not confront him or her and do not ask for group intervention, involving other people – this will just backfire on you in a big way.

Much as you want to warn others about this person, don't do it. The sad thing about it is, a psychopath is so adept at spinning tales and turning truth and accusations into an attack against you that you will wonder what has hit you, will be left wondering why it happened to you. You started out as the good person, just wanting to warn others and now you are the bad person in all this.

Get a Support System

While you cannot use anyone else in your pullback from a psychopath, you can get professional help in the form of a counselor or a therapist who is highly skilled at understanding and dealing with psychopaths. You will need someone in your corner, someone who is going to keep your focus on your health, in as physical and psychological sense. Should the psychopath refuse to let you walk away, it's not going to be pretty or easy to deal with by yourself.

You could try and draw your friends in as your support system but the psychopath may already have got to them, spreading accusations and lies about you so that, by the time you need them for support, they will be thinking that you are the psychopath but will be too scared to confront you.

Make Sure you Protect Yourself

A psychopath will think nothing of draining you, emotionally and in terms of assets. That includes power, money, your status or your reputation. If they see you as a threat to the success of their existence, as a person who may be able to stop them from manipulating others, they will do everything in their power to destroy you and to see that you lose everything you own and everything you stood for.

They don't need your things but they won't see you have them either and want nothing more than to see you destroyed, beaten down and left with nothing. This is their demand – the price they want from you if you want them to leave you alone. Do not allow it to happen. Do what you can to protect what you have left.

If you have a really good job, schedule a chat with management and explain the situation you are in, tell them that you have left the relationship and are trying to cut all ties. Be honest about the entire situation. This is prevention – the psychopath may try to get you kicked out of your position at work, a common attack and, if your managers have been warned in advance, they are less lily to believe stories about you stealing, using drugs, having an affair with another employee. These are all the sorts of stories that a psychopath will come up with to try to get you discredited.

As soon as the psychopath realizes that you are going out of your way to avoid him or her, having no communication or interaction with them, they will start bad-mouthing you to anyone who will listen, especially if they think you have realized that they are a psychopath. In very rare cases, especially where you have only just met, and they don't feel that you are any kind of threat to their existence, they may just allow you to go, without another word.

Don't Give In

Stick to your course of action. If the psychopath counter attacks do not, in any way, respond to them. If you say even one word to them, it must be something that you are prepared to stick to and you must show them that you can no longer be manipulated or goaded into attacking back, regardless what they say or do. Keep your head up, your back straight, a smile on your face and a positive outlook, show that you are full of confidence, even if you really are falling apart inside. If they see even a chink of weakness in that armor, they will find their way back in and attack you again. Do your falling apart in private, out of sight of anyone else and then put your confident face back on when you face the world again the next day.

Preserve your Reputation

If you still have a reputation left, do everything you can to preserve it. A psychopath has a very good ability to turn opinions of other people their way and away from you. Don't take it personally – again, I know this will be hard especially if they are people you thought of as friends – and, although it will be hard to lose support of these friends and your family, you must remember it is not their fault – they have been taken in the same way that you were.

A psychopath will do all he or she can to save face. The must always be seen as the victim, never the victimizer and they are very happy to take on the task, regardless of the reputations they will destroy in the process, in order to hold on to the position they perceive that they hold in society.

Be Prepared for the Absolute Worst

A psychopath is going to use every word you have said against you; they will use your actions against you. Expect it. Be prepared for it. There will be verbal attacks, defamation, claims that you set them up, you trapped them, anything to show them in a good light and you as the psychopath. Be prepared for an attack to come in any format – it may be verbal; it may even be via the internet. Be aware that if you use social media sites, your friends and followers are the perfect target for a psychopath and he or she will quite happily launch a full-scale social media war against you.

Document Absolutely Everything

Where possible, keep hard copies of evidence, statements made by the psychopath, letters, emails, and attempts to contact you and keep it all in a safe place. Make copies of everything and store it in another safe location, two or three if you can. That minimizes the chances that the psychopath can find and destroy the evidence.

Be very careful what you say to the psychopath. Act as though you know that everything is being recorded and may be used against you in the future. Do not say anything that could possibly be spun completely out of contact and made to make you look like a psychopath.

Maybe, in time, the people you used to know, those who you considered to be friends and trusted, will come to see the truth: you were telling the truth all along. However, be aware, the psychopath is so clever and a master at manipulation that, even after his or her true colors have been revealed, those people will still wonder about you. Don't hold on to any hope that one day you will be vilified of the accusations that were hurled at you. You may want to consider looking for a new set of friends...

Do Forgive Yourself

It was never your fault that you were conned by the psychopath, that you believed everything that they said to you that's what they do. You are the victim here, not the perpetrator and you may just have found yourself in situations that you couldn't get out of. That doesn't make you an idiot or a fool. A psychopath can draw anyone in and it happens to all sorts of people from all walks of life every day of the week.

You had no way of seeing the train wreck that was heading your way, no way of avoiding it. Bear in mind that some psychopaths will target you, wait until you are at a particularly low or vulnerable moment in your life and then move in for the "kill". Learn from it. You know the signs now, you know what to look for and maybe you can help others to see those signs too.

# Chapter 8: Who Is Reliable, Anyway

Have you ever been sick?

When you are on your own, if you are sick you have to get on with it. You eat what is in the cupboard, you rest, and you hope that you will get better soon. If things get really bad, you might call a relative, or a friend, or an ambulance. That's pretty much how it goes.

When you get sick and you have a dependent in the house, it is a little tougher because you still need to feed your child, or get your kid to school and back, etc., so there is no shame in asking for help. In fact, you should, before things get really bad.

When you are with another adult in the household and you fall sick, you are not expected to get on with it without help, to cook or to drive others, or to have to call for help to a relative, a friend or an ambulance yourself. If you do, something is not right.

In a partnership, the normal thing is to rely on your partner when you are down. If you can't rely on your partner when you are unable to function, take this as a sign of imbalance in the relationship.

This could mean many things, though.

Maybe you are taking upon too much, and need to start easing down a little. Maybe it's not a very serious relationship and one, or both, of you are only in for the fun times. Maybe is just a case of bringing perspective and figuring things out together... In other words, it doesn't need to mean that something is terribly wrong, but it is definitely a flag that something is not working and needs to be fixed, because if you can't count on your partner, you are effectively alone.

And also bear in mind that when it comes to bad relationships, not only you cannot count on your partner, but you can count on your partner making things worse, reason being, they are not there to make you happy or to do things for you when you most need them. Quite the opposite.

Let's put an extreme example, say that you have to be hospitalised for whatever reason, and your partner tells you to call your mother to take care of you, so you can be in some capable hands and with minimal disruption on your partner's daily schedule.

If so far you don't see what's not right, let's take this a little further.

So, you are in a hospital bed, in pain, worried about what's going to happen to you, dealing with doctors on your own, with no support, and having to consider to bring your mother into the picture, of course having to arrange the whole thing by yourself and without your partner's further input.

Now tell me something, what is the difference between being on your own and being with a partner of that sort?

I'll tell you what is the difference:

The amount of disappointment and extra worries when you least need it.

In a nutshell, you want to be with a partner that is reliable and can get a handle on things when you can't. You do not want a partner that tells you to sort it out from your hospital bed.

And when this happens, when your partner let you down when you most need him or her, it really doesn't matter how much you think you love this person, or loved this person up to this point: This is not something that you are easily going to forgive and forget.

I understand that many decades ago calling a relative to take care of you and cook for your husband while you were poorly was a practice considered quite normal. However, this is the thing: Neither you nor your partner was part of that generation. You were both born many, many years later, when women already had the right to earn money, and vote (I know, right? Crazy stuff).

So no, calling your mum to take care of you is not the sort of things that you would do, unless strictly necessary and for reasons that were completely out of both (your partner AND your) control. And you would do it as a team, and for the purpose of causing minimal disruption to your kids, for instance, not to your partner.

That's it.

And that is the true meaning of Reliability in a relationship:

To be able to count on each other to go through challenges together.

It is not about dumping stuff on your partner, it is about figuring things out together. If you can't do that with your partner, you won't make it as a couple.

But don't worry, you don't need to wait until you are in hospital to find out if you made a mistake by staying in the relationship.

Once you are aware that you both need to rely on your better halves for some things or others, it is really quite easy to spot when that is not the case.

Think about the definition of the word:

Reliability (noun)

The quality of being trustworthy or of performing consistently well.

—Dictionary Definition.

Now, can you trust your partner to do things for your relationship, your common home, you, or your children, and do them without your having to step in? Or do you feel that it is all on you?

Did you discuss and agree to that?

The reality is that if you can't trust them, imbalance occurs. But why can't you trust them?

This is a brilliant question to spot whether you are being played, or you are doing wrong.

Think about these case scenarios:

If you are being told that you are too controlling, and need to back off, back off. See if your partner does something or nothing.

Is your partner using the old trick of the timestamp to procrastinate?

Is the result different but works? Or is it just ruined or left unresolved indefinitely?

If your partner assumes that this issue is your job or responsibility, question yourself: Did I agree on this being my responsibility?

If you need help, and your partner is not stepping in to help, think: 'What do I do when it is the way round? Am I doing all the things and getting nothing in return?'

In any given situation where your partner needs help or there is shared responsibility, any normal person would react by either stepping in and doing their part, or simply stating some ground rules and clarifying what they are not prepared to do and why. You may or may not like the outcome, but that is a different matter altogether.

What really is the issue here is that you can reason with normal people and come to an agreement that you can count on that it will be respected.

However if that is not the case, if what happens is that they make up all sorts of excuses to not step in, do whatever badly and then turn things around and blame you for it, they are effectively making things worse as opposed to consistently well. At this point, they become untrustworthy because they are unreliable.

It is also unreasonable to expect no support from your partner, no matter the excuse.

For instance, I think one of the naughtiest excuses I have ever heard was 'I'm not like you, I can't multitask!', talking about cooking and clearing the kitchen. Basically this man was playing the "Women can do more than Men" card, and trying to pass as a victim of circumstances.

I know that there are women out there that will believe they have some sort of gender supremacy, because as we live in a society that values us less, systematically, the only way they feel reaffirmed is by going to the other extreme and proclaim themselves better.

We are talking about people that believes that the term Feminism is equivalent to some obscure proclamation of women supremacy, as opposed to the actual definition of the word:

Feminism (noun)

The advocacy of women's rights on the ground of the equality of the sexes.

—Dictionary Definition.

I feel it is unfortunate and ignorant, for anyone, to believe in gender supremacy, but it happens; and if such a person is in a partnership with a player, that card may work because at that level of ignorance reality checks will be deliberately ignored.

At the end of the day, we live in the Information Era, where we have access to all sorts of data for free, where knowledge is available to everyone with an android phone, where we no longer need to study a career to know about stuff, and where ignorance is a choice.

That argument of multitasking would be a really difficult one to argue, if women are expected and believed to be able to fry the meat and to wash the frying pan at the same time, rather than in turns, and for free, simply for the pleasure of catering and amusing their partners.

Fortunately, some of us do accept that we do not have such super powers, so that gender card will not go down well on us, and it will become apparent that we are being taken for a ride, and again for free, because I for one wouldn't mind to take on that duty given a fair salary, a reasonable amount of days off, and good working conditions.

But going back to the original point, this was an example where this person (A) is being relied on for cooking meals and clearing up, without agreement. And at the same time, (A) cannot rely on partner (B) to do it even occasionally. (A) not only has to ask, but also gets an argument each time from (B).

Now, is it only the cooking and kitchen clearing, or is it the shopping, the washing, the ironing, etc, as well? Is (B) doing part of the work? Which part?

The reality is that if (B) is holding (A) responsible for the whole lot of it, (B) could be assuming the role of an eternal guest in (A)'s home. And it is (A)'s home because (A) is the only one making it so.

In terms of extra work, less time for anything else, and potentially the added expenses if (A) does not receive any money for all the work, who can afford an eternal guest? And let's not forget that nobody starts a relationship to gain a guest, because that would be plain crazy: (B) is clearly taking advantage of (A).

It can also happen that (B) is holding (A) responsible because (B) is paying most of the bills. But this sort of agreement needs to be worked out, it can't just be assumed, because that would mean that (B) does not want a partner: (B) wants a butler.

Either way it is unhealthy, and the unavoidable will happen: (A) will loose all attraction to (B).

Unfairness is not cool, and it certainly is not sexy.

Reliable is the new sexy.

Mark my words: If you cannot rely on your partner, the sexappeal will gradually disappear, simply because:

Who has the energy after all that daily unrewarded effort and disappointment?

And why would you fancy anyone that is continuously disappointing you?

The Danger of Agendas

Something else to consider is, people with hidden agendas.

Hidden agendas mean that the person following them may or may not be relied on that particular day, or time, but that may change at some other day or time, who knows.

In other words, the person with the agenda is still unreliable because you never know when or if you will ever be able to count on them. Hence you will still be disappointed at them, and, because of their position, you will take on a bigger load that will impact you negatively, again, bringing imbalance to the relationship.

On top of things, if you are dealing with an abuser it is really difficult to realise the imbalance because:

It all comes ever so gradually.

There are always great excuses for it to happen.

You are so busy with all the things dumped on you that you simply do not have the time nor energy to question them.

This is why you need to make a point to stop sometimes and think: 'Do I go out much?', 'Do I see my friends regularly?', 'Do I exercise sometimes?', 'Do I get Me time?', and 'Does my partner do any of it?'

It doesn't take long to question, and it is good and healthy.

Now, if only one of you do all those things, there is an imbalance: One of you is relied on too much, something needs to change.

Let me give you another example, a day to day one: Say that you are working late, and you are starving when you get home, only to find your partner starving too.

Any normal adult that feels hungry at home can do a number of things, like a sandwich, or calling you to check if it's worth waiting, or just make dinner.

It makes sense, and depending on your dynamics as a couple, you can rely that the other person will do one of them. That would be normal behaviour.

But say that your partner was busy with whatever, and didn't think of doing any of those things. Again, normal would be proposing a take away, or sandwiches for both, or cooking something quickly. In other words, taking his or her part of the responsibility on providing with dinner, showing that even if it isn't perfect, you can still rely on them to be able to feed themselves, and hopefully think of you too.

And let me point out here that this is how you can spot when something is utterly wrong: If they make you responsible for the lack of dinner, starve themselves unnecessarily and blame you for it, with still no dinner plans on sight, you need to realise that dinner was only an excuse to create a problem.

Reliable is who sorts things out.

Unreliable is who doesn't.

Abusive is who creates problems and uses them to argue, blame you, and make your life as difficult as possible.

The point is that as an adult, and a normal person, you need to be capable of sorting things out. But to be able to do that, you need to take responsibility, which means that someone that does not feel accountable, will never be reliable.

You can't expect someone to take responsibility for something they don't feel accountable for. They might help you or not, depending on their motivation of the day, but that's all they are doing: Helping (or not helping) you, because they hold you responsible.

It is impossible to rely on someone who does not take responsibility.

And that is The Hidden Agenda: You can't rely on them, they rely on you; this is because you are the one taking responsibility for both, which is what they were after in the first place.

So of course somebody like that will think that dinner is your responsibility, not theirs. And no, they won't feel that they have to fix what they feel that you messed up.

Instead of fixing the issue, they might give you a nasty argument for not doing dinner (the aggressive partner), or they might ask you what to do (the helpless codependent), or they might just expect you to sort it out, since that's what you do (the passive). And the bottom line remains the same: You are the only reliable one in the relationship.

All their weight is on you. And if you react to it and protest, they will not understand why, simply because they truly believe they don't have responsibility on the matter.

This is not a recipe for a happy life together.

You both need to be reliable. It doesn't work if at least one of you is not reliable.

There is no balance in that, there will never be.

So think about it carefully:

Do you have a partner, or have you adopted an adult?

And please pay special attention on how responsibility shifts crucially depending on the answer.

# Chapter 9: How To Handle Sociopaths

When the word sociopath is mentioned, a number of people often think about a serial killer. While it is true many serial killers are sociopaths, there are more of them leading normal lives, leaving very little room for anyone to suspect them. Chances are that more and more people know them as citizens leading ordinary lives. However, this is untrue because they do not actually lead ordinary lives since they do not have a conscience. They do not have empathy neither do they feel any affection towards others. However, a number of them can mimic feelings and can therefore pretend to be loving and very affectionate.

Since sociopaths are pretenders, they often go undetected until they are firmly in one's life. If they happen to be a spouse or a workmate, they can easily wreck havoc on a family or a workplace because they are often discovered when it is too late. They hardly ever feel sorry for their actions and wish to take anything they want without the slightest care of what happens to the others.

Sociopaths have sharpened their wits at deceit and lies. They also manipulate their victims with the aim of only fulfilling their desires. After getting into someone's life, they leave behind them a chain of destruction, confusion and hurt without being remorseful. When confronted, they make the victim appear like the villain or seek sympathy to be allowed back to someone's life.

The toughest part in handling a sociopath is actually accepting that that person you are in love with, or a friend is a sociopath. Most people prefer to sweep the truth under the carpet rather than attack it head on. Here is how to know you could be dealing with a sociopath;

Uses you most of the time.

Does not care about you.

Lies and deceives you.

Makes contradictory statements.

Takes more from you and does not give back.

Makes you feel sorry for him or her.

Feels bored most of the time and wants stimulation.

Flatters you to get something from you.

Blames everyone and everything other than himself or herself.

Makes you feel like you owe him a lot.

If someone does all these more than every other person in your life, you are dealing with a sociopath. Research shows there is no known therapy or cure for people who behave this way. In fact, there is evidence that it could only make them worse as they use therapeutic sessions to learn more about human nature to exploit them even more. Many of them do not seek therapy and if they do, they intend to gain from it. This is how to handle the person:

If the sociopath is a spouse, it is better to run as far away from them as you possibly can. They usually have a tendency of following their victims and this means you need to be too far away.

If the sociopath is your friend, child or sibling, turn down their unusual requests and do not show sympathy. Be as indifferent towards them as they are towards you. Imagining that you can heal them is a real waste of time. They are usually beyond help.

Be firm- Sometimes out of sympathy, people are bound to relent a little. Once they are aware there is a way they can get your sympathy, they often exploit them. Refuse flat to give in to their demands.

Sever all links- In case they knew your bank details, or anywhere else you had property, change all that. To get to you, most of them try to hurt you using every means available; including destruction of your property. Keep them out of his/her reach.

In the event that you have children, they may try to get them or harm them to get to you. Seek police protection and try your very best to keep them as far away from you as you can. In case they have the rights to visitation, ensure there is protection around you and the kids whenever you meet.

Of course it is not easy to be callous towards the sociopath, but the right step has to be taken to get them off your life to give you room to move on. It is tougher if it is your own child. But you need to turn down their endless needs without budging.

# Chapter 10: Bipolar Ben

You've been dating Ben for quite some time, and you can tell that you have had your share of ups and downs. By ups and downs, you are referring to his moods — he tends to be so happy and excited about the future, and then become depressed and self-loathing the next. You are becoming increasingly worried about him and your relationship — ever since he started having these mood swings, you have been feeling like you are walking on eggshells, afraid to trigger his foul mood. You feel inadequate and helpless, but you know that you have your great times together and you do not want your relationship to go to waste. However, you are beginning to doubt your ability to handle this relationship, and you are beginning to also doubt if your efforts are going to be enough. You are starting to feel inadequate. If only Ben remained happy, positive, and optimistic, everything would be fine.

The Swings Of A Bipolar

Ben is most likely to be suffering from a bipolar disorder. Most people tend to dismiss it as mere mood swings, but it could possibly be a lot worse. It is very confusing for a person to be extremely happy one moment and then extremely sad the next without a particular reason. Because bipolar disorder has a lot to do with hormonal imbalance and pent-up stress, people who are struggling with it may feel that they have to rationalize their moods swings whenever they occur. They often feel misunderstood and they often have to hide their feelings, which make their conditions worse.

However, people around them also feel as confused as they are. You may realize that you are losing your own patience and you feel that every happy smile and sudden tantrum thrown at you is a test on how long can you keep up with the intense mood swings that you have to deal with. You may feel that your emotions are being toyed with and it makes you feel that you are not doing your best, even if you are already doing everything that you can.

When you look at how bipolar disorder affects both the bipolar and the people they have a relationship with, you would see that everything that you feel is just a misreading of the situation. It is not about you or the other person — you are dealing with a chemical imbalance, which can be resolved by medication and healthy lifestyle.

What You Can Do

The good news is that Bipolar Disorder is highly treatable with counseling and/or medication. Living a healthy lifestyle also plays a big role in managing the frequency and intensity of manic episodes. The best course of action for a person like Ben is to first seek medical help. Seventy percent of people with Bipolar Disorder respond well to medical treatment. However, be cautious when you mentioning medical treatment to Ben — some people would deny that they need help or believe that they can live through the situation without being treated like a patient. If Ben does not want to see a psychiatrist to help him battle bipolar disorder, do not push it. Instead, encourage him to have routine checkups instead.

Also keep in mind not to take any of his emotions personally during his manic and depressive states. Remember that this is not about you — he is undergoing confusing emotions and surges of strength because of what is going on inside his body. What you can do is to make sure that you draw the line on how you are going to react during his mood swings and how you would normally behave when you know that he is himself. You would also want to reduce stress and triggers of stress and make sure that he is getting enough rest, especially during his manic periods.

While you would want to support a loved one who is battling with bipolar disorder by making him feel that you are with him in his journey to recovery, you may also need to seek personal support. Dealing with another person's struggle with bipolar disorder can be very difficult and emotionally draining and you need to have the means to release your own tension as well.

Also remember that you need to prioritize your own life — there is no way that you can enable yourself to support a person struggling with a bipolar disorder when you cannot provide for your own needs. It is going to be a tough ride through the mood swings and working to stabilize them, but you have to hang in there.

# Chapter 11: Sociopaths In A Family

You have to understand that some sociopaths form some sort of attachment towards a group though generally they exhibit no emotions. Sociopaths may be attached to their siblings, partner or children. This is a peculiar behavior shown by sociopaths. This is one reason why you will hear contradictory versions of a sociopathic person when you talk to different people. A family member may call him very affectionate and loving; while at the same time people at the office may find him devoid of emotions. It therefore becomes difficult to identify a sociopath. In the absence of consistent behavior, you may never know whether someone is a sociopath.

A sociopath may not form any emotional bond with his family or any other group. It is not necessary for a sociopath to show emotions to a specific group. Since the prevalence of sociopaths is quite high (one in four), there are many families with sociopaths living among them. Such relationships are cold and emotionless. Sociopaths go through the motions when conducting social rituals. They are essentially indifferent to their family members. Such behavior may also go unnoticed when the family is living in poverty or other challenging situation. Emotional wellbeing among family suffers greatly in such a situation.

If the response of sociopath were lack of emotion alone, it would not have been as serious as it is. Sociopaths show total disregard to the safety and security of their family. They may put them in dangerous situation because they themselves lack the power to discriminate between good and bad. Reckless drunken driving, dangerous outings involving accidents and exposing children to unwanted television serials meant for adults, like pornography, are some problems which families of a sociopath may face.

Sociopaths never compromise or adjust to their partners. It is either their way or no way for them. In such circumstances, it becomes difficult to maintain relationships with them. Co-parenting with a sociopath is almost impossible because they do not understand responsibility. The manipulative behavior of a sociopath can compel them to treat their children as possessions. They may love and cuddle their children at one moment and be dangerously demanding at another. The children, in such families, turn out to be maladjusted and show behavioral problems.

Overall, the behavior of a sociopath in family setting cannot be predicted. They may be loving and caring towards some specific members of a family but detached and emotionless with others. You will also find sociopaths in a loveless relationship. Sociopaths, in general, cannot form long lasting family relationships. They may be part of a family which is dysfunctional because of the individual of due to some challenging circumstances where the family is required to compromise or reconcile to a situation.

Lack of social etiquette is another sign of a sociopath. They can get angry and violent in situations which do not warrant such extreme behavior. The situation can get exacerbated if the person facing the sociopath tries to be logical. It is better to leave them alone in such circumstances.

# Chapter 12: Psychological And Clinical Assessment Criteria

Psychology can credit Hervey Cleckley with the first clinical assessment criteria for psychopaths. In 1941 he published a book, The Mask of Sanity, where he tried to provide the clinical community with a way to diagnose psychopathic patients. He created a checklist with 16 characteristics devised after numerous case studies with psychopaths and he further revised his checklist four times in almost 50 years of experience with clinical studies. Here is the list of the 16 characteristics:

● Absence of delusions or irrational thoughts

● Superficial charm and normal to high intelligence

- Unreliability

- Absence of "nervous" behaviors

- Untruthfulness and insincerity

- Inadequately motivated antisocial behavior

- Lack of shame or remorse

- Poor judgment and a failure to learn from experience

- General poverty in major affective reactions

- Pathologic egocentricity and incapacity to love others

- Unresponsive to general interpersonal relationships

- A specific loss of insight

- Fantastic and uninvited behavior with/without drinking

● Impersonal sex life with poor integration or trivial feelings for it

● Failure to follow life goals

● Suicide is rarely carried out

Although suicide is rarely something accomplished by a psychopath it has been seen in sociopathic behavior to some degree. A mass murderer discussed in famous sociopaths named Applewhite is a perfect example. He not only had many followers who committed suicide, but committed his own right along with them. For psychopaths suicide is not usually carried out because there is a lack of empathy and remorse. The person is more likely going to get a thrill from seeing mass suicide that they created rather than following their prescribed thoughts on the matter.

Cleckley was the first to create a checklist for clinicians and psychologists to follow.

However, it was Dr. Robert Hare who modified the checklist adding four other traits. The Hare Psychopathy Checklist-Revised is used today by psychiatrists, psychologists and other experts of the psychology field. When courts are dealing with a psychopath usually an expert who can properly interpret the checklist is called in and will testify to avoid any issues with improper diagnosis or sentencing. Given the different terminology Hare used to create the checklist they will all be listed below:

- Superficial charm

- Grandiose sense of self-worth

- Pathological lying

- Need for stimulation

- Conning and/or manipulation

- Lack of guilt or remorse

- Shallow affect

- Parasitic lifestyle

- Callous/lack of empathy

- Poor behavioral control

- Impulsive

- Promiscuous

- Lack of realistic goals

- Early childhood behavior issues

- Irresponsibility

- Short term marital relationships if any at all

- Failure to accept responsibility for actions

- Revocation of conditional release

- Juvenile delinquency

- Criminal versatility

The information was supplied by PhD Kent Kiehl's book, although it is available online with similar terminology. These checklists are those with the rating 0 through 2 as mentioned in the previous chapter. When a patient is rated if the characteristic does not count, a 0 is assigned, whereas a 1 is used if it partially applies, and 2 is if it fully applies. A score of over 30 means an individual is a psychopath. As you can see both lists have very similar concepts, while Hare's full checklist offers a few more considerations to make. Everything from the checklist to the DMS V information mentioned in a previous chapter is used to determine the score a person has on the checklist and for psychopathic, sociopathic, and antisocial personality disorders.

Clinicians are taught how to assess an individual in different ways than you may be thinking. For most people it is about instincts and assessing certain characteristics. A lot of it can be hindsight when someone they knew is arrested and suspected of criminal activity. For clinicians it is not about the offense that client is currently being convicted for or incarcerated for. Instead, it is based on the personality of the person which is assessed through questions. The score received should be the same regardless of the crime committed.

Criteria to determine antisocial personality disorder, psychopathic, and sociopathic disorders for clinicians are all the same. It has to be. A standard has to be provided as a means to uncover the truth; however, for psychopathy it is slightly different. There are additional tests the go beyond psychology criteria found in a book or through Dr. Hare's checklist.

Referencing CAT scans and MRIs again, you should already understand that the brain of a psychopath reacts differently to certain images in which feelings such as empathy or guilt are typically the ideal response. Dr. Kent Kiehl is a leader in the current MRI studies of psychopathic brains. He has taken numerous prisoners' brain scans through being able to bring mobile MRI units into prisons. He has further been able to map more brains for psychopathic studies for the future of determining how to treat psychopaths. Unfortunately the same cannot be done for sociopaths.

Treatment

A silver lining with sociopaths and other antisocial personality disorders is treatment. Psychopaths are not receptive to treatment. They do not admit guilt and trying to analyze the brain and adapt behavior through therapy treatments does not work. It can work for antisocial personality disorder and sociopaths depending on when the treatment is provided. Despite the option of using therapy for treatment, it is not always successful. The deeper the scars are for a sociopath the more difficult it is to use therapy as a treatment. This is particularly true in the case of criminals. Sociopaths who have already made it to the stage of committing atrocities have gone beyond therapy treatments and often when released from prison commit new crimes.

Regarding treatment, there is a chance for a solution just not at this time. Treatment for individuals with sociopathic and psychopathic tendencies is still focusing on psychological therapy. To a degree this can help individuals traumatized in childhood, but the patient has to want the help. Sociopaths and psychopaths that are able to function or at least do not commit violent crimes have found therapy to be successful. All though no one can understand why the violent streak is not universal to all with antisocial personality disorders, it is at least comforting to know that certain individuals can get help and do go in to treatment.

A key difference with those who seek treatment is they are unaware of the true problem. Some have gone in to treatment for depression thinking it is their lack of ability to maintain goals and hold long term goals. Others consider self diagnosis without having a second opinion to corroborate their beliefs.

For violent offenders with known psychopathic tendencies linked to brain activity, the judicial system is still trying to work out how to prosecute and treat these individuals. The chance that they will be released from prison after serving their sentence or gaining parole only means there is a potential to commit new atrocities as has been seen in historical cases. Yet it is against their human rights to be locked up on what might happen if the judiciary system allows release. It is also a question of whether the person is capable of being on trial as a sane individual.

MRI studies are helping to indicate if there is a known problem with the MAOA gene and other genes linked to psychopathic behavior as a way to diagnose and prove that while the person knew what they were doing there were medical circumstances. The argument is not for these individuals to be released from prison, but for leniency in sentencing for states with the death penalty.

The medical studies with numerous MRI scans of psychopathic brains have one goal—to find a way to correct the problem. Therapy as a solution does not work, so figuring out medication or a way to produce the enzymes necessary to feel guilt, remorse, empathy and love are also solutions that have been discussed. At the moment there is still a large whole in how to correct the issue.

It takes time and it is dependent on the individual with psychopathic tendencies. Forcing medication is illegal. Even patients with schizophrenia can elect to take their meds or not. For the safety of others and the patient those with schizophrenia who are unwilling to take their medication can be committed. The same may eventually occur for psychopaths, where a known danger to others or one's self will allow for a family member to commit the patient and have medical rights. However, until a proper treatment can be provided for psychopathic patients there is no real answer in how to deal with those who are sane, but lack the ability to feel properly until they commit a crime that requires legal action to be taken.

# Chapter 13: Are You Killing Your Relationship With Passive Aggressive Behavior?

Passive aggressive behavior is the kiss of death to open communication.

Saying things like "fine, whatever" or "go do what you want, I don't even care" with a clear tone of disapproval are often part and parcel with the passive aggressive arguer's method of expressing their disapproval. Guilt trips, saying one thing but meaning another, and faulting people for not doing what you want but not expressing what you actually want are also all highly passive aggressive.

It must be said first that breakups are not usually the fault of only one person in the relationship. To get to both the beginning and the end of a relationship, both people played a role in some way. However, it's often not the person yelling loudest who is actually subtly killing the relationship.

There are fewer things in the world more difficult than having a discussion or argument with a partner who is passive aggressive. At the core, the entire reason behind an argument is to sort out an issue with a partner. It is often necessary to argue occasionally, to get feelings out on the table and actually improve the relationship. If you shut down, become passive aggressive and start undermining the other person's attempts to change the communication, you are doing both of you a disservice.

The other issue with passive aggressive behavior is that it tells your partner that you can't get past your own hurt feelings to make an effort to improve your relationship with them. It signals to them that you're not willing to honestly lay your feelings on the table and improve the relationship. This hits to the core, because if you don't want to improve your relationship, then what are you doing there in the first place?

While your underlying intention with passive aggressive behavior may really be to avoid confrontation, in the long run you're causing more harm than good. Here are two of the main reasons why.

Passive Aggressive Behavior Forces You To Bury Your Feelings

If you're not sharing how you really feel with your partner, but still holding them responsible for hurting you, you give a lot of your power away. You are keeping your expectations for them a secret but expecting them to somehow read your mind and figure out what you want. That is like calling a plumber and then saying "I don't know, fix it!" when they arrive. Your partner isn't a mind reader. It isn't fair to try to please a partner who will only show disapproval when you screw up.

Then, to add to it, the disapproving partner says "EVERYTHING IS FINE!" They clearly are not fine, otherwise, why would they be pouting and shouting? This is a minefield that your significant other may eventually tire of crossing.

Passive Aggressive Behavior Stops Productive Communication

When you have stopped telling the other person what you would really like from them in a clear and nonjudgmental way, you stop productive communication. It's important to remember that your partner is not a mind reader. They shouldn't have read only non-verbal cues to figure out what you want.

Finally, passive aggressive behavior breeds resentment in both partners. The passive aggressive partner feels like their needs aren't being met. The other person feels like they have to run backwards through a forest to figure out what you really want. Neither position is a good one to be in.

To keep things on an even keel in your relationship, practice being gentle but clear about your feelings and expectations. Don't fault the other person for not knowing rules that you haven't explained clearly. Remember that the real goal here is to improve the relationship, not make the other person feel bad.

CAN A PASSIVE AGGRESSIVE MARRIAGE BE HEALED?

Passive aggressive behavior is relatively common, and includes sabotaging behaviours intended to establish a wedge of separation between both of you. Look at this list, and see how the end result is isolating the husband from the marriage, from the spouse and finally from his own feelings.

In this way, he reaches the point of hostile dependency, where he feels not tied up to an emotional relationship which risks making him feel dependent on other.

This is the perception of the spouse of a passive aggressive husband:

Agreeing to do something and then accusing me of being demanding when he doesn't do it.

Saying one thing, doing another and then denying saying the first thing.

Changing minds about what he is going to do frequently.

Not showing interest in others.

Displaying bitterness and jealousy at other's achievements.

Not accepting responsibility for anything that goes wrong.

Continually complaining about not being appreciated for working so hard for the family but not really working any harder than anyone else.

Mumbling so she can't be sure of what has been said.

Obsessive interest in internet and other distractional things.

Distant and "busy" even when in the same room, so avoiding connecting with her.

Being one half of a passive aggressive marriage can be down right lonely and frustrating. You can't seem to get inside your spouse's head and understand what makes him tick.

What you see as right, he needs to say that he sees as wrong, and if you see something as a positive, he'll turn it to a negative.

Your husband may have developed this behavior from having an unhappy childhood. If his parents were ice cold, too strict, or abusive, he may have learned that it was a bad thing to express any kind of emotions. He could not show his emotional need of and dependency from his parents, for fear of being scolded and rejected as a "sissy." This leads to a lot of resentment and hidden anger, being expressed in a passive way later in his adulthood.

If you feel you are in a passive aggressive marriage, the best way to handle the situation is to be assertive in your communication with your spouse. Be direct with him while explaining your concerns. Assert yourself explaining the effect of his passive aggressive behavior on you; without blaming him or throwing guilt, explain what happens with you when he needs to show that he doesn't need you.

Be prepared to hear quite a few excuses, but don't let that side track you. Don't allow your husband to control you or the conversation. Find a way of calling him on his passive-aggression without being holier-than-thou about it.

If you are not extremely angry or frustrated with him, perhaps you can help him see the pattern, which is usually the toughest part. If you can explain the pattern to him just when it is happening and not be too judgmental, or taking him too seriously, that would help.

The whole psychological point of being passive-aggressive is to spare oneself the messy implications of experiencing one's anger. And it's not easy getting a grown-up man to say he's feeling like a child inside. Their feeling of repressed anger is so intense; it has never been dealt with in the family of origin and he could never bring it out, so it feels like a mountain of anger for him. Show him that is not such a high mountain and it can be demolished with support and humor.

If this man has the qualities you admire and love in a man, keep your cool and don't get frustrated by his passive aggressive behavior.

ANGER AND DOMESTIC VIOLENCE

People who are suffering from anger management problems are likely to inflict physical and/or verbal abuse on the people close to them, such as their children or their partners.

These people are suffering from antisocial disorders and personality disorders and they can also suffer form paranoia, schizophrenia, psychopathic disorders, histrionic, sociopath disorders, bipolar disorder, attention deficit disorder etc.

People suffering form these problems are passive aggressive and are prone to outbursts due to their lack of anger management skills and are very commonly abusive in relationships.

Anyone in this category is very dominant and, if the other person does not accept them as dominant, then they try to enforce their dominance with their behavior. This can be by inflicting their victim, which is most commonly their spouse, with physical, mental and verbal abuse.

People with antisocial disorders are often under the influence of substance abuse as well and have no regard for the rules and regulations of society.

These people have developed anger to such an extent that there is no way back for them. They are set in their angry ways and they are quite happy with what they have become.

They love to tease, humiliate, intimidate, abuse verbally and physically and feel happy and satisfied when they inflict misery on people around them. This is their form of anger management.

In social circles, these people project themselves as very cool and charming people and most of the time people are attracted towards them. This is the point where these people are falling prey to their angry mind.

With the outer charm and charisma of their personality they attract people, and when an association is made they reveal their sick dominant mind to the other person. If they face retaliation then they explode and inflict the full force of their anger on their prey.

In their rage and fury they can even kill people and they have no regrets, but may actually have the urge to kill again. This is almost their form of anger management.

There are many people around us who have such personality disorders so we have to be very careful when we make new relationships and should only make new associations with initial caution and care.

The majority of the time these killers are not caught by the police because the wildness of their anger is reserved for their prey. To the rest of the world they are as charming as ever. There are various serial killers who play with the lives of other people and they never accuse themselves of doing wrong or inhuman acts.

The anger of these people is most dangerous for other people because they have mastered their negative anger with their own form of anger management.

Even if their lives are anger driven they are in control of their actions.

In the end, I will just say to be careful in making associations with people who are antisocial and if you are in a relationship with such a person, leave him/her as soon as possible for your own sake and safety.

## TESTING ITS IMPACT ON MARRIAGE

We all begin experiencing love relationships by a strong connection and feelings that we are completely understood and accepted. Of course, this very deep feeling doesn't last, and sometimes we wonder: where did our strong and deep connection go? Is this happening to you now? Are you struggling to maintain the loving connection that you once had with your wife? Many relationships begin to flounder on rocky shores due to frequent miscommunication and opposing communication styles that go on unchallenged.

You may say or do one thing, which your wife misinterprets or doesn't understand at all, leading her to act in a rejecting way that is unsatisfactory to your emotional needs. If you feel your marriage is wrecked by fights and anger attacks based on miscommunication, it's possible that as a result you've been accused (more than once) of not being "open" enough with your wife, taking her for granted and/or hiding your opinions from her. She may have even used with you the label: "passive aggressive."

If that's all true, it's easy to see why you'd be reaching the limits of your frustration (or she is reaching hers). In situations like this, it can feel as if an irrevocable blow to the marriage is the only thing you see on the horizon: divorce. If this option is not what you want, if a loving marriage with your wife is what you truly desire to have but aren't sure how to achieve, we'd like to ask you to think deeply for a moment.

Isn't it possible that the traits in yourself that you call your "personality" reserved, brooding, emotionally and physically sparring with loved ones are not only causing problems in the relationship, but are not really your personality at all? What if those ways of acting that your wife has continually termed "passive aggressive" and "sabotage" are really behaviors that you've learned early on life or taught to your own brain without realizing it?

The answer will be hard to define because this is the only way you know how to interact with others. If this is not your "natural" (born with it) personality, how are you supposed to act instead? It may be a daunting task to look at this situation, but trust us, you cannot afford to put the matter to the side.

At the core of our selves are very basic human needs for love and connection. Often, neither party in a struggling marriage knows how to give voice to those needs and ask for a nurturing or fulfillment of those needs. Thus, marital grief can continue to escalate as long as one or more people (here, the wife) feel taken for granted and ignored. Even when it is a basic skill, partners need to develop a reciprocal atunement to the partner's emotional needs, in order to take care of providing satisfaction and emotional support and attention.

We know. It sounds like a simple enough approach: sitting down and analyzing yourself. But often, this is the hardest thing we have to do as humans! When you're feeling as if your wife is pushing you to divorce because of "strange" accusations, try to identify what inner forces are sabotaging your marriage. Your wife deserves a better marriage, but remember: so do you.

## WHY PEOPLE SABOTAGE THEIR LOVE RELATIONSHIPS BY USING PASSIVE AGGRESSIVE BEHAVIORS

In the glow of a new love relationship, our expectations of bonding, sharing and connecting with each other are very high... and this high feeling corresponds with the satisfaction of our human need for love and connection.

We are all programmed by evolution to search and find another human being to develop attachment to. There is a need to have someone to depend on, a loved one who can offer reliable emotional connection and comfort. In this search, we involve everything we have: hormones, our emotions and our personal life planning, given the importance of finding a good life companion.

Only afterwards, through painful disconnection experiences, we can begin to get painfully familiar with the little gaps and misunderstandings that bring us back into the loneliness of our individual situation, back from the unity.

This is part of the process, the step by step learning to share life with another person, which becomes a permanent task with its own rewards.

What happens when the other person, the person you have chosen to be your safe emotional connection, is not understanding the nature of developing a relationship? What happens when the other person involves himself into a cocoon of isolation and secrecy? And gives you only empty responses?

You begin to feel little by little pushed into a painful loneliness... most women talk about being stuck in a "lonely marriage," where they can't connect with their spouse. Usually, they complain about long periods of silence, secrecy, and in general an attitude of not sharing anything personal with them.

Even being involved in a good fight, their spouses would appear to handle conflict in a calm, detached way, but then later react in an uncaring or wounding manner to a calm, non-conflict situation, seemingly "out of the blue."

This response further damages the relationship because it causes confusion and pain to the receiving person and she cannot respond the way she needs to because she doesn't know what provoked such a reaction to begin with. And requests for explanations go unanswered... or can provoke long silence periods.

Why is this response happening? why do some husbands distort normal communication in this way? Basically, to protect themselves from what they perceive as an intrusion or an attack by their wives, misinterpreting a request for a deeper connection as a threat.

Passive aggressive behavior often stems from a deep feeling of insecurity in a relationship and the expectancy of rejection from the most important person in one's life. This perception of always being in an insecure attachment develops in early childhood, and persists as an unconscious expectation about relationships in general for the rest of our lives.

Attachments in general are seen as threatening inner balance, demanding impossible tradeoffs and exacting a high price... is a mostly negative expectation that transforms any little incident in a reason to withdraw emotionally and hide from the other side.

A person often develops this behavior as a defense mechanism, however ineffective, because needing to recover a sense of both protection and strength. Passive Aggression is protective because it shields the emotional world of the person in a silence cocoon, severing connections and preserving a sense of isolation.

It can be used not only as a protection from the assumed intrusions of the spouse, but also provides a way to retaliate against their real or perceived emotional threats. Long silences can drive the punished spouse crazy, without having a reason or a cause that can be improved or solved... simply, there is no explanation for the silence, but the excluded partner feels a terrible isolation and wonders why is the punishment delivered. Again, no explanation given, or a calm smile, or a "nothing is wrong" comment reinforces the isolation of the excluded partner.

Unfortunately, this type of behavior backfires because is most often used within close or loving relationships, those which present for this kind of immature partner with the biggest risk of loss, of hurt, of disappointment.

Because of this, passive aggression becomes a double edged sword because it turns the imaginary rejection risk into a reality as the hurt loved one eventually pulls away, reinforcing the fear and the secretive behavior in the person using passive aggression.

Still unsure about understanding what passive aggressive behavior is? Some more common terms that people use to describe someone using passive aggression are "backstabbing," "under-handed," or even "cruel."

Do these words pop into your mind when thinking of your husband or loved one? Or do people use them to describe you? If so, it's time to start learning more about why and how these behaviors happen, how to help someone with passive aggression, or get help yourself trying to survive a passive aggressive marriage.

Take steps towards helping your loved one, and helping yourself; do some reading, enlist the help of a relationship coach, get the support of your friends. There are resources available to you, and you need to understand this situation in order to be able to trust and love again.

WIVES SHOULDN'T LET PASSIVE AGGRESSION BRING THEM AND THEIR HUSBANDS DOWN!

It can take passive aggressive people years, even lifetimes, to realize the truth about the unintended impact of their behavior on loved ones. When they do, it often comes as a huge blow to see how they have hurt those they loved and maimed the relationships that were "important" to them, while they believed to be acting in a rational way.

They go from saying things like, "There is no way I can accept all this mumbo jumbo of PA... I can't deal with her complaining, and I think I have little to do with it. Why can't she shut up, appreciate what I give to her and live normally like other women do?"

To: "I have been married for 17 years and apparently slowly torturing my wife for all of them."

It can be shocking, depressing, frightening for the husband to see his actions and their consequences there in front of him. However, even after he realizes these hard facts, his partner definitely don't want his healing process to stop with "You're passive aggressive" and then leave him hanging. Nothing will ever change that way, and it may get even worse! The partner of a passive aggressive man should know that it's important that they remind him about the resources he has to have a better insight and stop his own passive aggression.

He needs to not only see his behaviors, and the consequences, but look beyond them to the solutions that can help his relationships recover. Think of it as a broken bone. First, you have to help the person see that their body is injured. Once they feel that pain and realize where it comes from, they'll want to heal and feel better! But they may need ideas about where the hospital and doctors are. They may need someone to lean on while they limp to recovery, too!

Although he may see his problem and want to solve it, he may also think, "I can't afford to help myself!" We're not suggesting expensive therapy as the one-stop, solve-all solution. Often, the best kind of foundation for healing will come from sitting down with himself and implementing strategies that make him look hard at his past and his childhood experiences. In many ways, real change is more like going to boot camp than therapy!

There are many resources out there for ending passive aggression (from the partner's perspective). But there are only one or two comprehensive guides for the men themselves. A great one can be found here, at Passive Aggressive System.

# Chapter 14: The Psychopaths: Main Characteristics And The Way They Operate

Psychopathic personality disorder falls under the category of antisocial behavior. We all have some antisocial tendencies. Psychopaths, sociopaths, and narcissists, however, have them to the highest degree. Although these three disorders are all antisocial personality disorders, they are very different. That being said, the psychopath is the most dangerous to society.

It is quite complicated to determine that someone is a psychopath. This is because they are aware of their antisocial behavior and are very good at hiding it. All antisocial behavior disorders start in early puberty. This gives the psychopath ample time to practice their acting skills. It is also during puberty that they realize their behavior is not normal and frowned upon. This discovery ensures that they are careful not to be discovered. However, they cannot hide their negative traits forever. Below are the main characteristics that will help you determine whether you are, in fact, dealing with a psychopath.

Outward appearance.

All psychopaths have the characteristics of being charming, intelligent and even popular. Most have good jobs and are capable of holding important positions in society. As they are able to manipulate other people, they can mold people's opinion of them to suit their needs. They may have many friends and acquaintances. This is all because they are great actors. They have deliberately learned to mimic the behavior of others. They can imitate gestures, facial expressions, and language to achieve their goals. To the psychopath, the only important thing is to get what they want at any cost.

Disregard for the law and authority.

While popular opinion is that all psychopaths are violent criminals, this is not true. Most psychopaths do not kill people, but may have broken the law is some minor or major way. This is because they have no conscience. While they do understand the laws, they have no moral code. If they feel they must break the law in order to get what they want, they will. They also feel superior to all and any authority figures. Some psychopaths never break the law in any way. However, even these individuals have a lack of understanding between right and wrong.

They lack many emotions.

Like narcissists, they lack empathy. However, it is on a much deeper level.

They do not understand human emotions. They may even be unable to recognize fear, pain or anguish in another person's face. They also do not feel many emotions. Shame and remorse are another set of emotions that they lack. That means they are incapable of being sorry. They may pretend to feel any one of these emotions to get what they want, but they are never genuine. Therefore, their behavior is a result of this lack of emotions.

They are methodological in their manipulation.

Once a certain level of trust is established, the psychopath will use subtle and overt manipulation in order to further his or her own self-centered agenda. Lying, which is typically incredibly easy for psychopaths, is the most common manipulative tactic. Often, the psychopathic partner will engage in cheating or sexual promiscuity, partake in reckless spending or gambling, or abuse drugs/alcohol with a complete disregard for the impact of such actions. Meanwhile, the psychopath's partner is left in the dark as they are overcome with doubt, fear, and insecurity in their partner. To make things worse, the psychopathic partner will often feel justified in pursuing such actions, and if challenged, will lash out with physical or emotional abuse.

A person with psychopathic personality disorder plans their manipulation carefully. They will construct a set procedure to get everything they want. They have no regard for whom they may harm in the process. All people, other than themselves, are irrelevant. They also enjoy the power they have over others. Before they start manipulating anyone, they will discover this person's strengths and weaknesses. They will then use this knowledge against the victim. Nothing a psychopath does is accidental.

Their view of self.

These individuals view themselves as superior to others. The fact that they are usually successful only fuels this opinion. As superior, they believe they have a right to treat those beneath them how they please. In case they are wrong, they place blame on others. The fault can never be their own. This overconfidence may seem attractive at first, but soon it is seen as selfish.

Charm.

Commonly, psychopaths are above average in the "courtship" process. In the beginning of the relationship, psychopaths will trick their partners into thinking that they are principled, possess virtue, and carry a high degree of empathy for others. This facade is meant to gain a necessary level of trust from their partners, which will ultimately serve as the framework upon which the psychopath will abuse and hurt his or her lover. In normal relationships, this trusting bond comes naturally, and arises from a mutual appreciation for one another's strengths and desirable traits. In psychopathic relationships, this bond is entirely one-sided; the psychopath exploits the trust of their partner as a means to manipulate and control, and to satisfy the psychopath's twisted sense of ego and self-worth.

Physical or verbal abuse.

While there has been much research to support the fact that psychopaths tend to have a "shallow" emotional capacity, this doesn't mean that psychopaths are unable to experience emotions. It's important to remember that, while they often lack empathy, psychopaths tend to experience a range of negative emotions such as anger, rage, jealousy, fear, and insecurity. While everyone experiences these emotions to a certain extent, psychopaths often use them as a means of not only gaining power over their partner, but also justifying their abuse. In other words, while most people would feel a tremendous sense of guilt or remorse, the psychopath only feels righteous in his or her devastation. Manifesting in constant criticism or belittlement, overt put-downs, and abandonment, the psychopath breaks down his or her partner to the point of insanity.

Overall, psychopaths are incapable of maintaining a committed relationship. At the same time, their relationships can last long time. They have even been known to get married. This does not mean that those relationships are healthy or monogamous. They will maintain their charming facade to the public, but life at home will be very different.

Psychopaths pick potential partners that are emotionally unstable due to some sort of trauma. Not people with other disorders, but people who find themselves lonely or insecure. They use all their charm and ask as many questions as possible. This does two things. First, it makes the person feel valued and interesting, so they lower their guard. Second, it allows the psychopath access what the victim is looking for. This, in turn, allows them to become the perfect mate. A psychopath will usually pursue a few targets at the same time. Although they choose one that is the most useful to them as a primary mate, they rarely let go of the others.

When a psychopath has their grip on their victim, the abuse begins. This can be psychological, physical, sexual or all three. In the case of marriage, they will trap their significant other with children. They are not capable of any form of love, but will show affection sparsely to keep the other person at all costs. Even their sexual advances are simply to get what they want. Apart from meeting their needs, the psychopath highly values power and control. This affects how they behave when in romantic relationships. They manipulate and humiliate their partner in many ways to maintain control. They will isolate their mate from family and friends. This again preserves their control, but also shows the other person their power. This means that their lover will be unlikely to leave, as they have nowhere to go. Psychopaths do not have relationships to fill a void of any kind. Every relationship has its purpose. Whether with a friend, a wife or a child, psychopath views them as objects to be used.

A psychopath never ends one relationship without having another one reserved. They get bored as soon as the surge of dopamine, which is released in the beginning, subsides. That, however, does not mean they end all relationships quickly. They change many mates, but may have one constant relationship at the same time. In rare cases the significant other leaves. This is rare because the psychopath destroys their self-esteem and independence early on. When this does happen, the psychopath will stalk their ex-lover. They do not accept defeat and view this as such. Even if the antisocial individual was the first to leave, they have a tendency to return. They use all the tools they have learned while being with the victim to reconcile. Of course, they still have no emotions, so the abuse resumes quickly thereafter.

Unlike many other disorders, a psychopathic one cannot be treated. This is because they have a serious lack of emotions and morals. In order for a person to be treated, they must want to change what's wrong with them. A psychopath believes there is nothing wrong with them.

They feel the rest of us are weak for having emotions. Their only goal in life is to serve themselves. What they want and need is the only relevant thing in their lives. With that in mind, they are prepared to do anything to achieve these goals. They have no empathy towards the people they hurt. This means that they will continually abuse people in their lives. Their lack of caring leaves them cold and all the emotions they show are fabricated. This makes the psychopath dangerous to those they meet.

# Conclusion

Psychopathy is a personality disorder that is considered as the most difficult to treat and deal with. Contrary to popular belief, psychopaths are not only people who have criminal tendencies but they can look like normal and healthy individuals that you deal with every day at work. Psychopaths are very dangerous to deal with and once you become their target, they will do whatever it takes to destroy you. Never let a psychopath get the better of you thus it is important that you understand their behavior. Being able to spot a psychopath in a room full of people is your greatest weapon to avoid them.